DEDICATION

To my sons, who have been, and shall remain, nameless.

CONTENTS

ACKNOWLEDGMENTS

Despite their claims to the contrary, the following people were instrumental in the writing of this book. Many thanks to Jennifer Bengston, Mark Brown, Jim Callister, Teresa French, Bob Grauman, Ron Pitkin, John Rossi, Yvette Saleh, Julie Slezak, and Lisa Taylor.

The ~~Best~~ WORST Baby Name Book Ever

INTRODUCTION

When I wrote *Don't Name Your Baby* three years ago, I urged parents to take my advice and stop naming their babies. The way I saw it, this hideous practice had caused a lot of trouble for unsuspecting babies destined to grow up ashamed and embarrassed by their parents' lack of common sense. Boys named Eugene were guaranteed years of schoolyard beatings; girls named Gretchen, years of dateless school dances. And all because their parents were without the guts to simply withhold their names until the kids were old enough to choose one for themselves.

Then I grew older and wiser, and I began to understand what I'd been missing all along. The obvious fact, which had alluded my understanding for years, is this: it's not the names that are disappointing—it's the babies themselves!

The names are just a function of what's wrong with so many people.

Now I'm sure *your* baby will turn out to be special. I'm sure when they pull that little sweetie into this world, she'll look more like Angelina Jolie than Carroll O'Connor. Who knows, maybe your baby will end up saying his first words on the floor of the United Nations. Maybe he'll discover a new planet with his Fisher-Price® telescope or invent a new, highly efficient diapering system that will revolutionize the world of infant textiles. Maybe she'll be so cute in that pink baby bow that Playboy will offer you a down payment on future pictorials. But probably your baby will end up like most babies—cute, but helpless. Special, but as your aunt used to say, "Special in her *own* way." And down the road, everything regresses to the mean.

Most people are ordinary. That's what ordinary is—ordinary. If most people weren't ordinary then they'd all still be ordinary—ordinary would just be called something else. And although some people are extraordinary in a *good* way, just as many (if not more) are extraordinary in a *bad* way. That doesn't leave too many positively bent extraordinary people. With such a watered-down gene pool, of course their names are mediocre, boring, ugly, or forgettable. Most *people* are mediocre, boring, ugly, or forgettable; and their mediocrity, over time, can't help but rub off on the names.

Logicians would call my argument in *Don't Name Your Baby* a causal fallacy. Or to use the Latin, *Post hoc, ergo propter hoc*. I've assumed that just because something happens after something else that the first thing caused the second. But the fact is, people have been around longer than names of people. A dumb cat doesn't need a dumb name to be dumb—he does it fine on his own. And by the same logic, can I really assume that just because few (if any!) women named Candy have achieved executive positions, that somehow their names are to blame? Of course not! It's probably just the luck of the draw—or the fact that the sort of parent who'd name a kid Candy is unlikely to raise a CEO.

In fact, you can probably assume that anyone who'd name his kid Myron is going to raise the kind of kid who gets pounded at recess regardless of his name. Anyone who'd name his kid Chad is probably a snobbish jerk himself, so naturally Chad will end up the same. And Bob is boring, so it follows that the people who raised Bob were probably destined to raise a boring person, regardless of what they called him. They thought Bob was a terrific name because that's the kind of dull people they are. And so the cycle continues.

"The fault lies not with our stars, but with ourselves," someone once said. (I believe I heard it on a sitcom.) So besides making me seem more intelligent (assuming anybody ever reads this page), this truism also indicates that years ago people knew this and didn't tell us. Well, I'm here to tell you. Your name does not determine your future. You determine your name. (Actually your parents do, but I was trying for parallel structure there.)

And so it's with a sense of *realism* and with *no animosity* toward the act of naming that I write this book.

Don't Name Your Baby? Nonsense! Give her the worst, dumbest, most awkward name you can come up with. It'll probably fit her perfectly!

HOW TO USE THIS BOOK

Are you serious? It's a baby name book! How tough could it be?

Still here?

Okay, you want some directions? Here's what you do: First, buy four more copies of this book. Second, give them to your friends and instruct each of them to buy four copies for their friends. That's sixteen. Work it out on paper for them if you need to. Explain to them that if they buy this book before it goes out of print they'll be saving money from the markup that the book will surely demand once supply is limited. Then tell them that every purchase of the book makes its relative value rise, as more and more books are removed from the potential supply. So everyone that they can convince to buy the book is putting money in their pockets! Assuming that every purchase of this book increases the value 10 percent (a modest calculation, I'd say), that means that the people beneath them in the pyramid[1] are increasing their wealth and that of everyone above them in the pyramid[2] exponentially.

---

1. The word *pyramid* in this context does not constitute any suggestion that the buyers of this book engage in any "pyramid" or "pyramidish" scheme. Pyramid is used here simply to provide a clear image of what the "scheme" might look like.
2. This time, it might actually be referring to a pyramid scheme.

The Worst Baby Name Book Ever

Pretty soon, *The Worst Baby Name Book Ever* will be paying for itself—and paying for your penthouse in the Bahamas! Enticing, huh? A yacht in Ireland? A wife in Armenia? A toaster in your bedroom?[1] Extravagant? Well, it can all be yours! All you have to do is *want it badly enough*! Do you want it, reader? Then let's get out there and buy some books!

---

1. These results are not usual. Individual results may vary.

Girls' Names

Abby
A cute little name that not only sounds like "Tabby" but kind of feels that way, too. Babies with Abby as their official name tend to like playing with yarn.

Abigail
Originally the surviving Siamese twin of the famous pair Gertrude and Rea, of Gertrude and Rea and their Amazing Underwater Orchestra. When Gertrude disappeared after a late night of drinking, Rea continued the routine, retaining the "and" in hopes of someday seeing her beloved Gertrude again.

Adrian
Formerly a boy's name that sounded like a girl's name, now Adrian is also a girl's name that sounds like a boy's name. Fortunately, many Adrians take up cross-dressing so that no one feels pressured to identify them as either gender.

A

Adrianna

The female form of the name Adrian, which these days is *also* a girl's name. So one can only conclude that Adriannas must be particularly girlish—in a tea party, frilly dress way.

Agatha

Babies named Agatha enter first grade already wearing their prematurely grey hair in a large bun and searching for their sweet Tweety Bird.

Aimee

This is how Amy would be spelled if it were screamed by someone falling off a building.

Alex

As if it weren't undignified enough to name a girl in honor of a man (Alexander), this name just gives up the fight and takes the sex change.

Alexandra

For parents who would like their daughter's name to evoke the memory of one of history's most aggressive men.

Alexis

A name that when spoken sounds like a sputtering car trying to say Alex. The last syllable just sort of stumbles . . . out.

Alice

Strangely, here's a name that sounds prettier when mispronounced (try stressing the last syllable and giving it a long *e* sound). But intentionally mispronouncing a name is every bit as ridiculous and pretentious as smoking a pipe while swimming. Also, nobody likes anyone who insists that *others* mispronounce her name—so it doesn't look like Alice will be sticking around much longer.

Alicia

If Alice is such an ugly name, and I think we can all agree that it is, what makes a person think that changing the last letter to "ia" will make it any better? Of course, it does *sound* prettier, but in order to pull that off, the entire pronunciation has to change, too. Doesn't that seem like a whole lot of work just to use this name?

YOUR BABY'S SIGN

Babies born under this sign are fat and will need to wear a girdle someday.

Ali/Allie

An excellent place to drink, shoot dice, have sex with strangers, leave a dead body, bowl, rob somebody, sleep, or urinate.

Allison

This has its origin in a time when young men would simply take their father's name and add the suffix "son." In this case, the name apparently means "son of Alice." The situation that could have sparked this designation baffles scientists to this day. *One thing* is for sure, though: Allison is a boy's name.

Alyssa

As any fan of the Red Sox can tell you, "She's a real pissa', that Alyssa!"

Amanda

Since amandine food is that which is served or prepared with almonds, this name is an acceptable substitution for those parents allergic to peanuts.

Amber

Amber has preserved the blood of dinosaurs in the bellies of ancient insects. Amber has some pretty disgusting interests.

Amelia

Originally a man's name derived from the title for one who practices the ancient art of furniture rearrangement, or amelioration. Since most people of the Middle Ages had little or no furniture to rearrange, the name quickly went out of fashion. Years later, when little girls would imagine themselves employed as adults, they would use the title of Amelia to indicate a woman working at some sort of job for which a woman might actually be hired, obviously a useless or fictional one.

Amy

A little girl's name that most self-respecting women in business simply abbreviate as "A." when they want a promotion. Since many Amys don't actually grow up, but rather retain a kind of Baby Jane fashion sense while living in their parents' basements, this isn't too widespread a practice.

Andrea

A combination of the names Abby and Gail originally used to name an entertaining pair of Siamese twins, Abigail Spidertail, who entertained sideshow gawkers with their stirring performances of the two-person play *The Gin Game*.

Angel

This name is growing in popularity in human beings just as it is waning among felines. Angels themselves (the flying kind), however, are apparently so outraged by this trend, that, in protest, they are naming their own babies Person.

Angela

The female form of the male Angel. Since in English Angel is already a girl's name, Angelas tend to be absurdly feminine, sometimes to the point of being mistaken for drag queens.

Angelica

A ludicrously long, four-syllable attempt to squeeze one more name out of Angel. Rumored to be in the works are the five-syllable Angelicatron and eventually the eleven-syllable epic Angelicardiovascularina.

Anita

A ridiculously oxymoronic name in that it means "little Anne" yet is actually one letter longer than Anne. Oftentimes this name is chosen by parents who, after having already chosen the name Anne, are astonished to find that babies are really small.

Anna

Very similar to, but just a little better than, Anne. Implies a sense of insecurity on the part of the parents and a naïve ignorance as to how many ways Anna can be rhymed with "banana" by a pimply faced eighth-grader.

Annabel

For parents unsatisfied with Anna and who'd like a little extra touch of beauty karma, just jam a "bel" on the end of the name. Of course, most Annabels believe that their parents will never appreciate them for who they are, and they express this anger in various self-destructive ways, such as having relations with married men and frequenting tanning salons.

Anne

Most girls named Anne become clinically depressed when they find that 50 percent of girls have Anne for a middle name—and usually because their parents couldn't think of anything else.

Annika

Most famously the name of Annika Sorenstam, who courageously proved that women are just as able as men to dress poorly and waste $100 a day on a good walk spoiled.

April

An excellent choice for parents who give birth in the spring and are entirely without imagination.

Ariel

The little mermaid. This name is most often chosen by parents who've conceived in a hot tub.

Ashley

Adverb, indicating an action completed in a manner either composed of or resulting in ashes, usually as a result of a burning cigarette on the person of the subject, as in, "Man, Dante really ran Ashley!" which, in this case, would imply that as he ran, Dante smoked a cigarette which dispersed ashes in his wake.

Ashlyn

A word originally used to refer to the smoldering remains of girls named Lynn who had been sacrificed to the god of suburban subdevelopments, Culdesac.

Asia

Not so much a baby name as it is a huge continent on which nobody is named Asia.

Aubrey

For girls named Aubrey, a much larger problem than the name itself is convincing teachers that they don't have a speech impediment and they *do* know how to write the letter *D* correctly.

Audrey

Girls named Audrey are just fine until the day they finally encounter girls named Aubrey. At that point they become intolerable, as all their suspicions that they are the perfect girl are confirmed.

Ava

Baby's first words: "Dahlink, I loff you, but give me Pahk Avenue."

Bailey

In reality, not a girl's name at all, but rather a hilarious nickname given to those prostitutes frequently arrested and bailed out by their wisecracking cell mates.

Barbara

Not a big French elephant or an uncomfortable undergarment, but an actual name—a name that guarantees the worship of young homosexual men around the world.

Becky

Officially naming your kid a cute, child-like derivative of a serious adult name is a sure way to make sure she never grows up, never gets a job, and never moves out of your basement.

Beth

Of the many derivatives of Elizabeth, this one is most popular among drug users because of the ease with which it can be transformed to the uproarious nickname Crystal Beth.

Bethany

Not really one of the fifty derivatives of Elizabeth, but rather a name of an Old English town that never existed. Pranksters in the sixteenth century would affix bumper stickers to their carriages that read "Bethany University" and strike up conversations about this fictional school at stops during their travels. Many such pranksters were beheaded for this sort of behavior.

YOUR BABY'S SIGN

Warning: Babies born under this sign cannot be bribed with a Happy Meal.

Betty

The only derivative of Elizabeth that actually smells like pot roast.

Bianca

Means "white." Although most girls named Bianca are in fact white-skinned, the name is not the exclusive property of white people nor any of their many subsidiaries.

Blain

Odd, but true definition: A blain is a swollen, puss-filled sore. Revolting name, huh?

Blair

If your baby's gonna be a screamer, then no name would fit better for the little loud mouth.

Bonnie

Besides sounding like "bunny," which is an association that doesn't inspire much hope for success, Bonnie bears the distinction of being the only Irish name that non-Irish people have no interest in using.

Brandi/Brandy

A beautiful name whose very mention will sound a reminder of shame and misery for every alcoholic relative she will have.

Breanna/Breanne/Breanon

Pick one of these names and nobody will know how to
spell or pronounce your daughter's name for fear of
choosing the wrong derivative. As a result, she will constantly be referred as Hey! and You There!, until one day
she'll just ditch the name you gave her and go with Yo.

Brenda

A brass bra of a name. Punch this name in the gut. Go on,
don't be afraid. Brenda can take it. Take Brenda with you
when you go into bad neighborhoods and if someone
starts trouble give 'em a face full of Brenda. That'll shut
'em up for a while.

Bridget

Although many people find this name exotically French, it
is really just "bridge" with a "t" at the end.

Brittany/Brittney

Oops. You did it again. Certain names just get stolen out of
the whole game, and this one's gone. Girls named Brittney
might as well be called Elvis for as little sense of personal
identity as they'll have for the next ten years.

Brooke

Girls named Brooke tend to babble like complete idiots. Take a good look at the baby (or just use the sonogram). Does she look . . . not too bright . . . kinda dim? This could be her name.

Cadence

Not really a name so much as "a progression of chords that seems to move to a harmonic close of point of rest."[1]

Caitlin/Caitlyn/Kaitlin/Kaitlyn/Katelyn

A PLAY

The scene: a soccer field. The audience sees the rear of four minivans, each of which seats a soccer mom at the wheel.

Minivan #1: Oh my God! Your baby's name is Caitlin?

Minivan #2: No! Where did you hear that? Her name is Caitlyn.

Minivan #1: Oh, thank goodness, because we already have two Caitlins on the block.

Minivan #2: I know! What a scandal!

---

1. Source: *New York Public Library Desk Reference*, 2nd edition.

Minivan #3: No, the scandal is those poor triplets who were *all* named Katelyn. Did you hear about that?

Minivan #4: Oh, that's ridiculous! Where did you hear that?

Minivan #3: It isn't true?

Minivan #4: Of course not! No decent hospital would allow such a thing.

Minivan #2: So what *are* their names?

Minivan #4: Kaitlyn, Kaitlin, and Katelyn.

Minivan #1: Just goes to show, you can't believe everything you hear.

Minivan #3: Point taken.

Minivan #2: Score, Caitlin! Score!

Minivan #1: I *think* you're cheering for the wrong side again, dear.

Minivan #2: Oh my. How embarrassing! Sorry. Score, Katelyn! Score!

Minivan #3: Block her, Kaitlyn!

Minivan #4: Pass to Caitlyn!

Minivan #1: Catch it, Katelyn!

All Minivans: Way to go, Katelyn/Caitlyn/Caitlin/Kaitlin/
Kaitlyn!!!

Callie

A name that is either misspelled or mispronounced—historians have yet to sort it all out. Girls named Callie disproportionately end up in speech therapy programs learning how to correctly say such words as *ball, fall,* and *call.*

Camille

French for "camel." Insert hump joke here: _____.

Candace

A difficult name. As soon as Candace has a friend close enough to call her by a nickname, she'll try Candy, and at that point the friendship will be over. Consequently, most Candaces tend to remain friendless and unmarried.

YOUR BABY'S SIGN

HOTEL

Babies born under this sign often grow up to be callgirls.

Candy

A terrific choice for parents who would like their daughter to end her ascent of the corporate ladder on the first rung. Most Candys get married when they come to realize they stand no chance of ever making a decent living.

Cara

Feminized version of the term "car." Cara is shorthand for any automobile that only women would drive, such as a Sebring convertible, a Volkswagen Rabbit, or a Toyota Tubetop.

Carla/Karla

Female version of the name Carl—a name so frumpy and unattractive that a female version had to be created so as to more accurately name frumpy and unattractive girls.

Carly

Adjective. Of, related to, or containing Carl-like properties, as in, "That girl dresses so Carly." Thus far, nobody really knows what that means.

Carmen

A name that referred to those men who would drive or park one's car, what we now call valets or drivers. It also is tied to the Norse combination of Karl (man) and man

(man) so as to create a double man, or as the Germans would say, Überman! In Basque, it might mean Chalkmen, which was a pale-skinned, power rock trio of the sixteenth century. An interesting choice for a girl.

Carol

An old standby of the middle twentieth century, you could always count on a Carol when you ran out of all the other names you really wanted. A haggard veteran of the name game, Carol would come in and get the job done. Rumor has it that Smithsonian soon will be including a Carol, along with girdles and iron lungs, in an exhibit dedicated to quaint and useful items of the twentieth century. During Christmastime, Carols are everywhere. Sometimes they even show up uninvited at your door. Frankly by January, everybody is sick of Carols.

Caroline

Here's an interesting fact: the name Carol is actually a derivative of Caroline, not the other way around. Caroline is a French, feminine construction referring to King Charles. As such, most Carolines are disliked by Americans, who, despite finding them sexy, also find them rude, unwashed, and unable to defend themselves.

Carrie

A homonym of the technical term for "tooth decay." Translated in Greek, the name means "deathy." Psychotic parents and those particularly fond of the Goth craze feel comfortable with this choice.

Casey

A terrific name for a girl! In the tradition of the manly "Casey at the Bat" and the tobacco-smoking "Casey the Engineer," this is true tiara for your little beauty.

Cassandra

Greek for "that crazy b***ch." The raving madwoman of Troy, who was actually right about everything she predicted. Sadly, nobody ever listened to her, so whether she existed or not is fairly inconsequential.

Cassidy

A Gaelic name that means "curly." Fans of the Harlem Globetrotters love this name and often choose it for twins along with Meadowlark.

Catherine

The Starbucks of names. Classy, popular, and, in various forms, everywhere. Also, much like Starbucks' baristas, Catherines expect tips for doing something as simple as pouring you a cup of coffee. More than a few Catherines are bitter and really ought to be returned.

Celeste
Refers to the dead rocks and balls of burning gas that surround us daily but only show themselves at night.

Chastity
A terrific name until young womanhood, when so many Chastitys experience intense feelings of shame and depression while engaging in their earliest sexual encounters. Fortunately, most Chastitys settle into lifelong frigidity to avoid having to experience such trauma ever again.

Chelsea
Old English for "chalk" or "chalkplace," where soft, gray limestone grows from the shells of little amoeba-like creatures called "foraminifers." Pretty disgusting, huh?

Cheryl
The French expression meaning "elaborate chair."[1] For those planning to give birth to an ottoman, this is an excellent choice.

---

1. This definition cannot be verified and in all likelihood is false.

Cheyenne/Cherokee

There's just something so arrogantly chic about naming your child after an entire nation your country eradicated.

Chloe

From the Greek goddess Chloris who personified Spring. Apparently, "chloe" might have been the sound she would make during a particularly exciting cross-pollination. Can you guess another word that might have come from this goddess's name?

Christian

A person can go his entire life and never meet a Buddhist named Buddhist, or a Hindu named Hindu. Thus, it is presumed that this name resulted from a nervous father filling in the wrong blank on his daughter's birth certificate.

Christine

The female version of Christ. This name will be especially useful when Jesus' sister is born.

YOUR BABY'S SIGN

Babies born under this sign will be liberal.

Cindy/Cynthia

Neither Cindy nor Cynthia like each other. Cynthia finds
Cindy frivolous and irrational, and Cindy finds Cynthia a
little too serious and totally pretentious. Such schisms
often create in girls a kind of split personality that men find enticing, but ultimately
terrifying.

Claire/Clarisse

Many parents go to this name because of its traditional fla-
vor but end up regretting that decision when they learn
that Claire means "famous."

Claudia

The female version of Claude, retaining all of Claude's ugly
awkwardness and none of his daring, devil-may-care-how-
ugly-my-name-is-ishness.

Cleopatra

Taking vanity and pretense to a new level! You'd better
hope she's good looking; otherwise, the irony will be
enough to ruin her life. Of course if she is like the historical
Cleopatra, she won't stay with a guy long enough to find
out what he thinks of her.

Coco

A real time-saver for people who own monkeys. If both baby and monkey have the same name (which is far less offensive than giving two babies the same name, Mr. Foreman), those confusing situations where you accidentally drop the monkey off at daycare won't be nearly so aggravating for providers who will now be able let Monkey Coco fill in for Baby Coco, without having to change any of the nametags.

Colleen

In Gaelic, this name is derived from the term "Irish girl," an expression used almost exclusively to refer to Irish girls, or at least ones whom sons would try to convince their mothers were Irish. It could also have been derived from the expression "Black girl" (from the Middle English word for black or coal, "col"). The expression "Black girl" may also have been used to convince mothers to believe in questionable ancestries, but with much less success.

Courtney

Derived of the ancient suburban expression, "Our daughter is 'specialler' than yours."

Crystal

A popular choice among today's most fashionable drug dealers, especially when combined with the middle name Beth. This name is so icy and cold that often boys on dates with Crystals find themselves suffering from frostbite by the end of the night.

Daisy

Most famously, the rage-aholic duck's enabling girlfriend who, after finally resorting to a restraining order, was able to get on with her life under a different name.

Dakota

Interesting evolution of this name: First, the name of a Native American people; second, the name of the virtually extinct Native American people; third, the name of a state; fourth, a name chosen for many dogs; finally, a name chosen for babies. Kind of like a neo-Nazi naming his kid European Jew.

Danielle

Originally a way to make boys named Daniel seem more French.

Dawn

In the days before electricity, Dawn was a rather important daily occurrence. Ancient civilizations saw Dawn as a monumental event that blissfully disproved their nightly suspicions that the world had ended. These days, Dawn is greeted with the horrible buzz of an alarm clock, followed by grunted cursing.

Deanna

Girls named Deanna insist that theirs is in the correct spelling of the ancient goddess of love. Nobody takes them too seriously and they often find their names at the end of sentences like, "Oh, shut up already, Deanna."

Deborah

The famous biblical prophet who roused the Israelites to conquer the Canaanites, whose name translates as "bee." Recent biblical scholars are floating the idea that the prophet Deborah was, in fact, a bee and that her prophecies really just amounted to a lot of buzzing and ass-shaking.

Deirdre

From "Deirdre of the Sorrows," who cried so much she put most of Ireland under water.

Deja

Why do I feel like I've heard this name before?

Denise

Most famously, the sister of Denephew.

Destiny

Yes, indeed, the Destiny of those who have unprotected sex is often the birth of a child. Really not too amazing when you think about it.

Diamond

Originally the name of a precious gem that carries with it a history of slavery, imperialism, and exploitation!

Diana/Diane

Originally shouted at viciously hated girls named Anna. Later in ancient Greece, Diana became a cute nickname for girls that every Greek girl hated. Finally, Greek men, knowing that the most hated girls were always the prettiest, began awarding the most attractive woman at the orgy the Diana Prize. From there, the rest is history.

Dinah

Hebrew for "vindicated," Dinah is the most popular choice among babies conceived during conjugal visits to penitentiaries.

Donna

Where Don means "man," Donna means "woman." While giving your child a gender-appropriate name is always admirable, to name your child Donna seems equivalent to naming a cat *Cat*. It doesn't show much imagination on the part of the parents. Girls named Donna tend to shop in the generic section.

Drew

The past tense of draw and a shortened form of Andrew. While the risk of a child mistaking herself for a verb is small, most Drews *do* believe they have been separated from a fraternal Siamese twin at birth and spend a great deal of time talking to themselves and researching circus life.

Dylan

The double whammy! Not only is it a radical, hip name, it's not even a girl's name! Oh, how girls named Dylan will be screwed up!

Ebony

A hilarious coup d'etat for the blond-haired, pale-skinned baby. They say that race doesn't matter? It will for her!

Those white families planning to have more than a couple of babies should definitely reserve this side-splitting prank for one of their girls.

Edith

Harkens back to a simpler day when mothers named their daughters Edith and laughed to themselves that even though they would die sooner than their daughters, at least they weren't named Edith.

Eileen

A side-splitting must for parents of babies born with one leg shorter than the other!

Elaine

French pronunciation of Helen. A name originally chosen by a French mother who, to this day, insists she told the nurse to write down "Helen."

Eleanor

A fun name to say out loud. Try it. "Eleanor!" Now try it with an English accent: "Eleanor! Get me my troubadour, Eleanor! And do something about that smellanor, Eleanor! Clean the door, wash the floor, and pile my pompadour, Eleanor!" What fun! Far more appropriate as a silly word than a name, though.

The Cult of Elizabeth

Years ago parents without imagination or basic spelling skills joined together to form a secret society known only as The Cult of Elizabeth. Lacking the ability to come up with interesting names for their group members, the Cult of Elizabeth agreed to simply name all members some derivation of Elizabeth.

This society doesn't do much, although they have been seen at Bennigans along the Northeast coast, watching reruns of *Friends* and doing shots every time Matthew Perry touches his hair. Witnesses have described the ritual as both mesmerizing and revolting. Some say they are all secretaries at an insurance company; others believe they are the true members of the famed "star chamber."

Their hierarchy is described on the opposite page.

"Elizabeth"

all members are ultimately responsible for her comfort and amusement

"Beth"

Responsible for purchasing beers for Elizabeth and making sure her lipstick isn't on her teeth; first in the long line of successors.

"Liza" (with a *z*)

Keeper of the cell phone and deliverer of instant messages; in the event that "a hottie" enters the bar, Liza is responsible for snapping his picture on the cell phone and immediately delivering it to Elizabeth.

"Lisa"

Keeper of the car keys and disher of the dirt; Lisa has vowed not to indulge in alcohol and to keep detailed notes on the private comings and goings of office personnel at Elizabeth's place of employment.

"Betty"

Dedicated toady of Beth; bakes homemade brownies every Monday and muffins on Friday to be delivered to Elizabeth but credited to Beth.

"Liz"

Dedicated toady of Liza; has been known to follow "hotties" home to snap pictures and gather information of girlfriends to be eliminated.

"Elsie"

A simple farm girl who apprentices for Lisa, learning the ropes of catty conversation and the physical mannerisms of discreet exhibitionism.

"Buffy"

Slays vampires.

"Bessie"

Elsie's cow.

Elizabeth

After all these years, this name still brings to mind the Virgin Queen who practically created the term "imperialism" and in the process created the term "hegemony" and eventually the slogan "down with all Westerners!"

Ella

The feminine suffix of many names, including Cinderella, Cruella, and Fella. As such, Ellas often report feeling inexplicably gypped, as if they've missed the best part of a movie and their very lives are simply the credits.

Ellen

An excellent choice for religious fanatics who want to name their daughter Helen but are uncomfortable with the whole H-e-l (-l) business.

Emily

A cutesy, little, scrunchy-faced name for girls whose parents think they might have given birth to a cat.

Emma

A simple name whose pronunciation requires no more skill than to open and close one's mouth. The perfect name for parents who are expecting an idiot-baby.

Erica

A refugee from those medieval days when girls were consider wasted births, and fathers would name the unwelcome newborn only in passing—usually by simply tossing a vowel at the end of the name they'd have chosen had they been lucky enough to have sired a boy.

Erin

Means "Ireland." Originally a product of a state-sponsored program in Ireland that granted the name of the country to families so poor they could not afford another name for their latest child.

Esther

Notable as the only name still in common use that easily rhymes with "the molester." The names Chester, Lester, and Hester seem to have vanished in recent years, showing up only occasionally on police blotters and neighborhood watch lists.

Eva/Eve

A popular choice in Bizarro World for girl babies born in the morning. Such girls live a topsy-turvy existence where black is white, up is down, and bran cereal tastes good.

Evelyn

A combination of the names Eve and Lynn, concocted based on the misconception that two boring names in combination create one interesting one.

Faith

Naming a girl after a virtue you treasure is a bit like the man who lives vicariously through his Little Leaguer. When that little shortstop decides he prefers soccer, or even sewing, to baseball, he's going to have a rough time readjusting his self-image, let alone that of his father. The world is full of faithless Faiths, trying to reconcile their names with their nihilistic lifestyles. And when they can no longer bear the shackles of their parents' dashed expectations, some can turn pretty ugly and violent.

Fawn

Girls named Fawn tend to be grating, little brown-nosers who try to get by on flattery rather than talent and hard work.

Felicia

Everybody likes Felicia. I know that if I were given Felicia (instead of my name), I wouldn't argue. So there it is: while not everyone likes giving Felicia, everybody likes getting some . . . it.

Fiona

A hilarious name to hear spoken by people from Minnesota and Canada.

Frances

While many people believe this name is the female version of Frank, it is in actuality simply the plural of France. Naming a child after a country is certainly strange, though not unheard of; however, naming a child after the *plural* of a country is just freakish. Of course, if this trend continues, be prepared to write out birthday party invitations to little Djiboutis and Burkina Fasos.

Gabriella/Gabrielle

In order to avoid having to say all three or four syllables this colossus requires, most of these girls eventually take on the nickname Gabby. As such, they become the nemesis of all the librarians and frazzled elementary school teachers they encounter.

Genesis

For people who want to show off their knowledge of the Bible, this one's a good choice. But if you really want to impress people, name your kid Deuteronomy.

Georgia

A former slave state that happily named an entire county after its most famous, violent racist. Babies named Georgia are usually covered in peach fuzz and bruise far too easily.

Gigi

A giggly kind of bouffant, high-heeled, tiger-skin-rug girl. Gigis are cute when they're little, but when they grow up, no matter how profound their contributions, they are not taken seriously. Gigis of the past may very well have proposed cures for cancer and designs for Middle East peace, but no one will ever know.

Gina

A partial name, more of a hint of a name than a finished product. Gina is like Van Gogh's *Starry Night* without the stars; like *The Wizard of Oz* without the wizard; like *A Farewell to Arms* without the arms.

YOUR BABY'S SIGN

Babies born under this sign tend to be fatter than other kids their age.

Ginger

Everybody's favorite sweet spice and spicy sweety on Gilligan's Island. It is well documented that not a man alive prefers Ginger to Mary Ann and among the reasons is her skanky name. Something about Ginger just feels like a venereal disease waiting to happen.

Giselle

Excellent choice for thin girls with long horns. Giselles tend to be shy, so approach their cribs slowly and hold out a sugar cube. This name is not a good choice for families who are planning on doing a lot of hunting.

Gloria

The religious equivalent of "Yahoo!" Most girls named Gloria say they appreciate the sentiment when everybody ritually and repeatedly sings their name every Christmas, but they also complain that it's getting a little old.

Grace

A hilarious name during those awkward years. Who hasn't enjoyed a good laugh at seeing a classmate named Grace drop her lunch tray or stumble getting off the bus? Choosing this name for a girl is a terrific way to bring those outrageous good times back home with you.

Gretchen

Most girls named Gretchen tend to be unusually attractive to compensate for a name that is so fantastically ugly.

Haley

Everyone looks forward to the arrival of a baby named Haley. Videotaping the event and then selling it to friends and relatives is an excellent way to celebrate and pay for this once-in-a-lifetime occasion. Parents looking to turn a profit might wish to consider t-shirts and key chains that read, "I saw Haley's arrival!" Who knows? They could be worth something one day.

Hannah

A name that forces a gentle rush of air across the lips as it is being spoken. Not a good choice for parents with a genetic disposition to chronic halitosis.

Harley

The brand name of a motorcycle noted for its paradoxical association with both fat, hard-drinking nihilists and soulless corporate posers who wish they were fat, hard-drinking nihilists.

Heather

A side-splitting hazard of this name happens when Heather's kindergarten scrawl is taken as "Heathen" by her teacher. Funnier still is when that teacher happens to be a heathen herself and, delighted to finally find a kindred spirit, befriends little Heather, taking her out to share lunch and a satanic ritual. Straightening out that mess can be one crazy time!

Heaven

A popular choice among people who apparently weren't aware that there already is a place called Heaven. And lately I've heard a lot of talk about potential copyright infringement suits being issued by its owners.

Heidi

Odd, but true: No one who has named her daughter Heidi has ever purchased a baby name book. Even considering the name implies that a parent is too far gone to be reasoned with.

Helen

Once associated with the most beautiful woman in the world, Helen is now a bit like the first car you owned: vaguely reminiscent of its former splendor, but mostly just an environmental hazard.

Hillary

This name had a brief spurt of popularity in the early nineties until the most prominent Hillary in the country actually suggested that she use her remarkable intelligence and prominent position for more than just baking and waving. Uppity babies who don't know their rightful place will like this one.

Holly

Every January, countless girls named Holly disappear as they are mistakenly packed away in boxes and stored in attics and crawl spaces. On a happier note, such families always seem to look forward to the annual "unpacking of the daughter" every December.

Hope

An excellent name for babies of desperately poor families, providing years of ironic hilarity as creditor after creditor remarks on their situation as "hopeless."

Ilene

This name actually began as the logical answer to the question, "What do you name a one-legged baby?" Ilene, indeed.

India

Not so much a name as it is a country wherein nobody is named India. Be prepared for plenty of panic and tears as little India overhears the news that Pakistan wants to "destroy India," and the international community will be looking for ways to "punish India." Night after night, news item after news item, opportunities will abound to discourage and frighten little India in these side-splitting moments of mistaken identity.

Iris

A popular name for children of optometrists that recently has been losing ground to other beauties like Cornea and Optic Nerve.

Isabel

I don't know what you're talking about! Is a bell what?

Jackie

Originally a way to show boys named Jack that you don't take them seriously, the name Jackie as a girl's name is used exclusively for baby girls who should have no expectation of ever being taken seriously. A good choice for babies who will be blonde, fond of horoscope columns, or shop at Bebe.

Jamie

A female version of "James," created when most people characterized females as silly little cuties, not to be taken seriously. Interesting fact: many mothers of Jameses refer to their son's penis as a Jamie.

Jane

Plain Jane. A terrific name for parents who expect very little from their daughter. Janes tend to mediocrity at just about everything they try. Eventually they just give in to domesticity—at which they are also mediocre.

Janelle

Another strange construction of the nineties where birth certificates for girls came with the first letter, a J, preprinted to speed things along. Most parents who choose this name say they do so for the sake of originality, yet it has become so popular so fast that it is now as common as the smell of urine in a city library.

Janet

A name whose very dignity was stripped from its chest during the 2004 Super Bowl. Under such harsh exposure, this name may not last much longer.

Jasmine

A name generally chosen under the advice of a doctor when it's discovered that the baby smells funny. The *name* Jasmine doesn't cover it up, of course, but it will provide years and years of ironic laughs.

Jenna

Two-thirds of Jennifer. An excellent choice for girls from whom you don't expect too much.

Jennifer

When making a list of the most popular girls' names in 1994, researcher Dr. I. P. Nightly found that during the month of March in that year *every single baby girl born in the United States* was named Jennifer.

Jessica

In the battle for supremacy over Earth and its simple-minded inhabitants, invaders from planet Jessicoid abducted and impregnated millions of mothers in the early 1990s, placing in them the subliminal suggestion to name their newborn girls Jessica. Today these young alien spawn populate our high schools, four or five to a class, awaiting the day when they will be commanded to begin the revolution.

J

Misspelled Birth Certificate?

You can't blame them. Long labors. Hospital bills. A new mouth to feed. It's a wonder more dads don't screw up when it's time to fill out the birth certificate! The real disaster occurs when other people upon meeting little Bichard and Racklyn actually think they've come across a winner. You want your kid to have a unique name? Try Mellonbutt or Garbageface. No one ever named his kid Garbageface.

But if you choose to call your kid Anfernee, don't complain to me when he flunks spelling.

Aubrey	Krista
Callie	Kiersten
Cally	Kirsten
Devin	Lezlee
Kayla	Tyra
Kelvin	

The following names are simply the babblings of fathers who were in too much of a post-labor stupor to utter anything intelligible at all.

Chloe	Ula
Dax	Uma
Deja	Una
Mia	Zoe
Tia	

Jessy

Your daughter's famous namesake: Jesse James, a homicidal bank robber who came to personify everything horrible about the American West.

Jill

Most famously, the idiot sister of Jack who, after seeing her brother go tumbling down a hill and sustain massive head wounds, fails to properly secure herself and consequently suffers the same fate.

Joanna

Originally the combination name of 1800s Siamese twin sensations Joe and Anna Kettlehack who toured the country as the highlight of Hefferman's Traveling Medicine and Trained Turkey Show. Eventually after falling in love and then seeing the relationship turn sour, the two suffered a horrible split from which neither would ever recover.

YOUR BABY'S SIGN

Babies born under this sign exaggerate about everything.

Jodi/Jody

The Joe of girls' names. Like Joe, Jodi is a pug-nosed, bald girl who looks more comfortable in a bowling shirt than a summer dress.

Jordan

A boy's name made so popular it blended into the list of girls' names when Michael Jordan dominated the NBA. Present stars will surely inspire the same sort of tribute and the tradition will continue as girls are named Yao, Carter, Bryant, and Mitumba.

Josie

A name that became popular in the early seventies during a time when young parents, still suffering the effects of hangovers from their drug-addled Woodstock years, began naming their children after characters from Saturday morning cartoons. Other popular baby names of the time include Witchy Poo and Hong Kong Phooey.

Joy

Ironically, most girls named Joy tend to be foul-tempered little brats who cause nothing but misery to everyone they know.

Judith/Judy

Despite the prevalence of nice booties among girls named Judy, most of them do not welcome the compliment.

Julia

Julius Caesar created this name for those frequent occasions when he would dress in drag (which in Roman times consisted simply of raising one's robe a bit) and perform at the local dragatorium.

Julie

A name originally coined by William Shakespeare in an early draft of *Romeo and Juliet* as Juliet's younger and uglier sister who, unable to catch the eye of Romeo, convinces Mercutio to kill him.

Juliet

Namesake of literature's most famous crybaby. First she doesn't have a boyfriend and she cries. Then she gets one and she cries. Then she gets married and stops crying for a while. Then she cries again. Then she dies. Then she stops being dead for a while, starts crying, and then dies again. What a drag.

Justine

A name that indicates "justice of the female sort." Such justice would include the end of Monday Night Football and criminal penalties for attending strip shows. A popular name among radical feminist lesbians who are adopting.

Kali

One of very few female names that seems more appropriate for a vegetable than a person. Thus, when Kalis introduce themselves, they often are greeted by more sensitive eaters with spontaneous vomit. In Hindi, Kali refers to a hideous, mythical character whose interesting fashion choices include a coat of severed human heads.

Kara

A handy name, easily pronounceable for those children born without lips.

Karen

An old standby, always willing to step in and take over when you can't figure out what to call a girl. Like an old station wagon or a straw broom, it'll get the job done.

Kate

For families without the means to acquire the multisyllabic Katherine, Kate is a terrific compromise. As an additional benefit, most Kates are perfectly happy to wear faux perfume and gumball machine jewelry.

Katie

Many parents, hoping to extend their daughter's childhood, will slap her with Katie, in the hope that Katie will play happily on the backyard swing set well into her thirties.

Katherine

A name that was created to better identify the meaner girls named Catherine. As such, Kathy then means "kind of fun, but meaner than Cathy."

Kayla/Kaylee

Names that just bring a perpetual smile to one's face. Kaylees and Kaylas, on the other hand, suffer horrible bouts of depression trying to live up to the perkiness expected of them.

YOUR BABY'S SIGN

YIELD

Babies born under this sign tend to give up too easily.

Kelly

The third choice of unimaginative Irish fanatics, behind Shamrock and Leprechaun.

Kelsey

Kelsey has such a good-time, barmaid sound about it that most Kelseys find they are unable to make it through college without becoming tremendously popular, tremendously fat, and tremendously alcoholic.

Kendall

A Celtic name that means "king of the dale." Yeah, king. Not queen.

Kennedy

A pathetically sad name for parents who feel no sense of importance in their own heritage and need to appropriate that of a mythologized American dynasty. About as pitiable as those guys in the eighties wearing cheap versions of Michael Jackson's red leather jacket.

Keri

A whispered shout. A slouching strut. This name is perfect for parents that want to feel like they've given their daughter an original name but don't actually want anyone else to know.

Kim

A name so boring that half of Asia stole it for themselves and nobody even complained.

Kimberly

When, in the mid-sixties, the name Kim was popular, the larger Kims separated themselves and became the Kim-burleys. Though the movement has ended, the name, in its present form, has remained.

Kirsten

An excellent way for illiterate and dyslexic Christian parents to honor Jesus in their own lovably mixed-up way.

Kristen

A word created by the Swedes to refer to the act of evangelizing door to door, as in "Sven! We're going kristin' this weekend! You coming?"

Kylie

A name that when pronounced forces the face into a look of complete idiocy.

Lacey

You'll want to avoid this name if your last name is Underpants.

L

Lakeisha Latasha/Latifa Latoya

Really just Keish, Tash, Tif, and Toy with a "La" and "a."
See, without makeup, even the most exotic specimens
look just like the rest of us.

Lara

A pet name for Larissa, Lara is the handy, easily pronounceable name for babies who plan to babble incoher-
ently into adulthood.

Laura

A traditional name that has done its job well since we first
asked it to travel west, leading the horses and taming the
land. Laura was there when the market crashed and when
we put a man on the moon. She did drugs in the sixties
and discoed till she died. That's right, died. We're only
propping her up now. It's time to put the old girl to rest.
Look at her. Isn't she as beautiful as the day she was born?
So long now, girl. You take care of yourself.

Lauren

Laura's evil doppelgänger, who, with a subtle shift in pronunciation, has managed to convince banks to cash her
checks and give her invitations to timeshare sales events.
This Lauren must be stopped.

Leah

Where the chastity of your daughter is concerned, naming her Leah probably doesn't help matters much. If she ever acquires the nickname "Easy Leah," it's time to change her name.

Leigh

See Leah. It's the same problem.

Leslie

A beautiful name for a girl. Often, if she is popular among the other girls at school, she will acquire the nickname "Lesbo." Then you'll know she's found herself.

Lily

To be lily-livered is to be perpetually scared, and to be lily-white is defined by Webster's as "favoring the exclusion of blacks, especially from politics." To be Lily is to start with a couple of strikes against you.

Linda

A flat-chested name with so little substance that it often needs to be written on the birth certificate twice.

Lindsey

For girls named Linda who just seem too fun for that name.

Lisa

One of forty-thousand derivatives of Elizabeth. Of them all, only Lisa is not taken seriously at all.

Lori

Lori, cooler than Laura in the way that Richie was cooler than Potsie—that is, not so much.

Lourdes

One of many places the Virgin Mary frequents. Although parents are certainly testifying to their faith when they name their daughter Lourdes, one can't help but see the hypocrisy in that none of the Virgin Mary's other vacation spots ever gets a kid named after it.

Mackenzie

Brings to mind that hilariously drunk dog! Boy, wasn't he funny, just sitting there while everybody else partied like crazy? What a dog! Yahoo! Before I write about this name, I have to have another beer. I'll be right back. . . .

Madeline

Just because some nurse believes that insanity may run in your family, does that give her the right to check a box that indicates to change your baby's name from Caroline, Adeline, or Lynn, to *Madeline*?

Madison

So many names have such exciting and exotic histories. This one begins all the way back in the grand old days of 1985, when in the classic film *Splash*, starlet Darryl Hannah first donned the name, chosen off a street sign. Such a lavish legacy to pass on to your little one.

Madonna

This is the kind of name that really confuses people. Literally translated as "my lady," Madonna supposedly refers to the Virgin Mary, but it's a different name entirely. Outside of the first two letters, the names have nothing at all in common. Furthermore, the performer Madonna has certainly appropriated the name for herself, so now trying to figure out the associations one ought to have with this word is enough to send a person straight to a confessional.

Maggie/Maggy

A name most famous for the song by Rod Stewart about an old, wrinkly, self-absorbed, obsessive tart.

Makayla

Kayla inexplicably rose to popularity in the late 80s even though it wasn't a name. Makayla is also not a name; in fact, it's a derivative of what is not a name. We look forward to the natural evolution of this name, Tippamakayla, in the near future.

Mallory

A beautiful name that means "bad place." As in the sentence, "Please save me! I'm trapped in a horrible Mallory, and I can't get out!" Horrible Mallory, indeed.

Mandi/Mandy

Scholars (or at least some guys sitting around watching television) speculate that Mandi was originally used as a term to describe ultra-effeminate men in the early twentieth century. Today, a metrosexual might be referred to as a Mandi.

Margaret

A difficult name to take lightly. As serious as a chandelier in an elevator, most Margarets have to grow into this name. Some girls, of course, deny their starchy destiny and choose instead to rename themselves Meg, Margo, Marge, Maggie, or even Peggy. Such girls find that they break their mothers' hearts in many other ways, as well.

Maria

After extensive testing, sociologists have found that—
despite the fact that this name has its merits—when saying
Maria loudly, there is no music playing. When said softly,
it's not at all like praying.

Mariah

A derivative of a name that itself is a foreign name, Mariah
is customarily pronounced so that the *i* is long, as if the
superfluous *h* somehow demands that.

Marie

Mary's hot little French sister. She can't cook and she
doesn't go to church, wash, or brush her teeth, but man is
she hot!

Marissa

A Poem for Marissa
I broke up with Melissa,
She wouldn't let me kiss 'ah,
Now I'm with Marissa,
And this girl's a wicked pissa'.

If You Don't Like Your Greek, Try Ours!

Name your kid after a famous person in history and chances are you're naming your kid after a pretty dubious character. You don't become famous by handing out apples for Halloween. There are only two kinds of famous people: saints and glory-hounds (a.k.a. jerks). The problem with saints is that their lives have been so scrubbed and canonized that your kid is bound to be stuck with a pretty high bar to live up to. Result: poor self-esteem.

So most people go after the legends of myth and history—the gloryhounds. Nowhere is that more prevalent than with the Greeks. Jason, Hector, Alexander: all of them jerks. But there are certainly famous Greeks worth a look. The names might not be pretty, but at least you're not honoring a dictator or a thief.

Instead of Helen, the world's most famous tramp . . .
• Try **Electra**, about the only person in her family who didn't kill anybody.

Instead of Jason, an adventurer who got tricked into killing half the world in search of an attractive scarf . . .
• Try **Oedipus**, a man who treated his mother well.

The Worst Baby Name Book Ever

Instead of Cassandra, who was a prophet taken less seriously than pet psychiatrists . . .

• Try **Iphegenia**, who was such an obedient daughter she let herself be sacrificed rather than embarrass her dad, a notoriously bad listener who misheard the directive, "The gods say you should *kiss* her" as "The gods say you should *kill* her."

Instead of Hector, who got what he deserved for ripping off Achilles' armor . . .

• Try **Prias**, who wet his pants hiding behind the walls of Troy while his son was carved up like a Thanksgiving turkey.

• Or try **Achilles**, a cross-dressing mama's boy with a tendency for 'roid rage.

• Or try **Ajax**, for a clean you'll really notice.

Mary

The Chevy of girl names. Just about everybody has had some experience with a Mary. For some of us, Mary was our first girlfriend just as Chevy was our first car. She kept us comfortable, and we kept her for a while. Then we grew up and tried some of those foreign names out. We even took a few spins with some real luxury models. But we all come back to Mary eventually, even if it's just in our memories. There's a Mary everywhere you look. And who knows? Maybe one day you'll get yourself one of these newer Marys. But what's the rush? Marys will always be there. They always have been.

Maureen

The feminine form of the insult "moron." Feminist babies prefer the gender-neutral "idiot."

Megan

A variant of the variant Meg, from Margaret. Most parents find that researching the convoluted origin of this name is a frustrating waste of time. Most grandparents find that attempting to figure out which of the millions of spelling variations the parents have chosen is just as frustrating and a waste of time.

Melanie

Roughly translates to Greek as "Blackie." Now Blackie is a pretty good nickname for a mobster and a terrific name for a dog, but not so great for a girl. But for those parents who were expecting a mobster or a dog, and instead got a girl, this is the most appropriate choice.

Melinda

Originally a combination name used as a means of self-identification by the cave people of ancient Europe. At that time, cave women would pound on their chests to identify themselves to other clans and say, "Me Grog," "Me Zuzu," or in this case, "Me Linda."

Melissa

Ancient Greek for "bee," Melissa is a sweet little girl name that, on a grown-up looks as strange as saddle shoes and black tights . . . just not as sexy.

Melody

Now, I know you are thinking of the beauty of Melody and how your little girl will embody all of this joy and grace. But not all Melodies are beautiful. In fact, some are down-right annoying. Take "It's a Small World After All" or "Macarena." They're Melodies. And remember that guy in *A Clockwork Orange*? Whenever he heard a Beethoven Melody, he'd go into convulsions.

Mercedes

There was a time that Cadillac was the best you could do. Then in the eighties, Cadillac became synonymous with everything that was wrong about American business: bloated, inefficient, and plodding. Right now Mercedes has an air of sophistication about it. Who knows, twenty years from now Mercedes may only bring to mind visions of German exploitation of slave labor . . . and the word "overpriced."

Mia

An incomplete name that was never meant to be taken seriously. The first father to write Mia on a birth certificate was intending something long and exotic, but just gave up when his pen ran out of ink.

Michelle

A French name that somehow held on to its original pronunciation during the journey across the Atlantic. With anti-French sentiment at an all-time high, and Congressional shame at an all-time low, bills have been floated in Congress to officially change this name to Liberty Shell.

Mindy

Mork's girlfriend. A woman who was so desperately lonely that she invited a manic alien to live with her.

Miranda

A Spanish word that was probably used to name the guy who would stand in the watchtower keeping an eye out for oncoming invaders. Unfortunately we'll never know since it appears that all villages who employed the term have vanished, probably as a result of being vanquished by invaders.

Molly

A real floppy-eared part-dog/part-girl name. Mollys have a hard time being taken seriously as beauty contestants, fairies, and princesses. They do, however, fit right in as housekeepers.

Monica

One supersonica name, Monica is the only name that rhymes with harmonica, gin and tonica, and all spellings of Hanukkah.

YOUR BABY'S SIGN

Babies born under this sign will need designated drivers.

Morgan

First women just had to vote, then they forced their way into college sports, now it seems that every time you turn around, a women is wearing a man's name. This one tends to look good on girls, but of course the novelty of wearing your boyfriend's shirts eventually wears off, and the next thing you know, you smell like a man.

Nancy

Bears the distinction as the only name in common usage that also exists as a term of insult. No boy wants to be called a Nancy. But simply because they are *not boys*, girls are supposed to happily accept the disparaging term as if it were a compliment. We should applaud the day when Nancys bravely protest their designation and gather to burn their birth certificates—and those ridiculous bows that bald Nancy babies have to wear.

Naomi

In a story that is as popular in lesbian wedding ceremonies as it is in syna-gogues, Naomi is the mother-in-law who convinces Ruth to shake her groove thing to get herself hitched.

Natalie

Most girls named Natalie are convinced by their parents'
choice of name that their birth was the ultimate event of
their lives and everything else goes downhill from there.
Sadly, it often turns out that way.

Natasha

Most babies named Natasha tend to be dark-haired, slow-
speaking double agents who prefer microfilm to rattles.
Mothers of Natashas, when leaving the hospital, are given
in their care package a capsule of cyanide . . . just in case.

Nicole

A French feminine version of the name Nicholas. Babies
named Nicole tend to smell, how do you say, *de j'ne sais
quoi*.

Nina

More of the end of a name than a name itself.

Noel

Children named Noel are often so closely associated with
Christmas that every January, thousands of Noels are accidentally boxed up with the garland and mistletoe and
stowed away in the attic for eleven lonely months.

Olivia

A female olive. Fun to press. Nice to have in the kitchen.

Opal

One of the uglier of the precious jewels.

Paige

From the Italian *paggio*, a word that referred to young *boys* in the service of knights. Were there female *paggios* or pages (and there were not!), they would be called *paggias*. So why do so many parents name their girls Paige? Is it because it's specifically a boy's title? Is it the servile nature of the job? Either way, it's a pretty poor choice.

Pam

Did you know that Pam breaks down if you turn up the heat? But if you can control it, cooking with Pam can really be smooth and easy. Be sure to dispose of Pam properly when you've used her up.

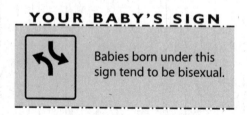

YOUR BABY'S SIGN

Babies born under this sign tend to be bisexual.

Paola

A name created as compensation for the Payola scandals that plagued radio stations and record companies during the fifties. Although reimbursing the artists who were unable to get their music aired during that time is impossible, at least they can receive some measure of satisfaction knowing that according to the settlement, every record executive has had to rename at least one daughter Paola.

Paris

Now here's a name that's gotten a little too much exposure the last few years. It seems like everywhere you turn, there's Paris. Paris is even showing up on the Internet a lot lately—so who knows, maybe we've seen too much of this name.

Pat

Things that like a Pat: a dog's head, a co-worker's shoulder, a mound of dough or dirt. Of course, many butts would appreciate a Pat, while many others (of the tighter variety) find Pats offensive. Give the president a Pat and you'll be tackled by the Secret Service. Pat answers are a sign of arrogance and rudeness. It comes down to this: if you want a Pat, just ask nicely. There's no need to give your daughter such a boring name just to get one.

Paula

Many parents believe they are paying their respects to the biblical Paul with this name. In fact, the name was first employed by parents who, after giving birth to girl after girl and having run through every derivative of Mary, finally gave in and tried a different New Testament name. Unfortunately, this family didn't have a great sense of aesthetics or imagination.

Payton

Surname of the greatest running back to ever play the game of football. Walter Payton, an inspiration on the field, as a humanitarian, as a father—a terrific choice of name for your little boy . . . wait a minute . . . you're thinking of using this for a girl? You've got to be kidding!

Penelope

This name won't be in the next edition of this book. I don't know how it got here.

Penny

The lowest possible denomination of money in the United States. Pennys are so without value that most people just dump the things into the "leave a Penny, take a Penny" bowl. In fact, the only reason anybody ever takes a Penny out of those things is to avoid receiving more Pennies as change. Nobody likes Pennys and we'll all be a lot better off when they're gone.

Priscilla

If names are dresses, Priscilla is a petticoat. Kind of a frilly, girly undergarment, sexy in a garish hee-haw way, but never anything you'd wear outside the house.

Prudence

Ironically, most girls named Prudence don't need to worry about this virtue since having such a horrible name so uglifies them as to never require that they refuse anything—nothing is ever offered.

Rachel

A serious name with roots in the stories of Jacob and Joseph, but with far greater significance for most Americans as the name of the girl in *Friends*. While most scholars believe it unlikely that *Friends* will still be influential in the distant future, scholars thousands of years ago said the same thing about that surprise publishing sensation the *Holy Bible*.

Raquel

Fifty years ago, Raquel Welch confiscated this name and placed it safely within her ample bosom. It has never been heard from again.

Raven

Yeah, okay, so your baby has black hair. Good for you. I'll bet she also has five fingers; how about you call her Quintidigit? Of course you won't. Doing so would show a complete lack of imagination. Kind of like calling her Raven.

Reagan

It is often unclear whether the baby Reagans have been named in honor of the former president or the split-pea spitting, possessed girl from *The Exorcist*. President Reagan babies tend to hate Khrushchev, and devil Reagan babies tend to hate Jesus.

Rebecca

Some people say this name means "noisy." Others say it is derived of the term "cattle barn." In fact, the name is really a combination of the two. Rebecca was the name used in ancient times to refer to the girl whose job it was to transcribe the incoherent ramblings of possessed cows.[1]

---

1. There is no mention of this phenomenon in any historical or biblical text.

Regina

Holds the dubious distinction of being the only girl's name that rhymes with that most private of body parts. Consequently, the name is intentionally mispronounced so as to prevent people from making the connection. What a horrible practice, to intentionally mispronounce one's own name. It robs a baby of any sense of dignity from birth.

Renee

The final two e's in this name are entirely mispronounced. As you can see, there is no accent above either e. Perhaps that is because English doesn't use accents!

Rhonda

A heavy, wobbly name that rests on a woman like a motorcycle helmet.

Riley

An adjective meaning to cause or to be in an agitated state. Colicky babies are often named Riley for their first year and then renamed thereafter.

Robin

Either a pet name for Robert or a winged creature who lives in grass and mud and eats worms, neither of which sound particularly ladylike.

Rori

An adjective to describe the call of effeminate lions.

Rose

Three Things That Dismay about Roses

One, the thorns beneath, you prick me.
Two, the bees that kiss, you stick me.
Three, they're ridiculously expensive. I mean, c'mon!
What do they last for, three days?
Roses suck. Forget it.

Roxanne

The Three Most Famous Roxannes.

1. The love of Cyrano who is so shallow she cannot see past . . . the nose on her face.
2. Sting's prostitute love interest in the song of the same name.
3. A late-shift waitress who calls you "honey."

Ruby

A derivative of the popular eighteenth-century name Buby, which did not survive the evolution of handwriting. Unfortunately, eighteenth-century *b*'s looked a lot like today's *r*'s (along the same lines of *f* and *s*). That's too bad, because girls named Buby were really stacked.

Ruth

While the book of Ruth is one of the most beautiful works in the Old Testament, Ruth's oath never to leave her mother-in-law has not survived the twentieth century's homoerotic test. Thus Ruth's oath is now most often quoted at lesbian wedding ceremonies. Now there's nothing wrong with that, but it seems to me you should let *her* make that call.

Sabrina

Most Sabrinas eventually get nicknamed "The Teenage Bitch."

Sally

A pig-tailed, knee-socked, bratty name that never seems right on an adult.

Samantha

A soft, classic, and beautiful name. Unfortunately, most girls named Samantha eventually take on the nickname Sam. At that point, they begin to take on male characteristics, such as mustaches and a rude habit of adjusting their "gear."

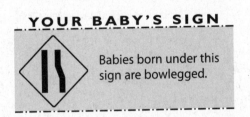

YOUR BABY'S SIGN

Babies born under this sign are bowlegged.

S

Names That Command No Respect
(or, Too Square to Be Hip)

While it is true that a commanding personality commands more respect than a commanding name, a goofy name just makes you look like a goof. And on that long climb up the corporate ladder, unless your kid has Bill Gates's charm or Paris Hilton's brains (actually, reverse that), they won't make it up too many rungs tripping over a goofy moniker.

Little known fact: Captain Kangaroo was overlooked for numerous promotions simply because of his ridiculous name. Even Albert Einstein, despite the validity of his many scientific breakthroughs, was known to have complained many times that he might have actually accomplished far more if he didn't have such an uncool name. Now unless your kid has an $E=MC^2$ up his sleeve, you might want to go with something crisp and classic, like Robert, Chad, or Alexis.

But stay away from the names that sound really cool to you *today*. Remember how cool the eighties felt in the eighties? Well, they don't feel so cool anymore, do they? Giving your kid an overly trendy name is like permanently

---

2. This isn't a footnote. It means *squared*, you idiot!

tie-dyeing him or sewing a Michael Jackson sparkly glove onto his hand, or sticking him with an eighty-year lease to a VW Bug.

When you're naming your kid Summer, you're only thinking how cute a little baby named Summer will be. And sure, Baby Summer's cute. But CFO Summer . . . well, CFO Summer doesn't exist and never will. When Chad comes into the boardroom, people pay attention. Xander just makes you giggle.

You can count on seeing your kids reside in your basement well into their thirties with these trendy, goofball names:

Autumn	Joaquin
Brock	Miracle
Caden	Serenity
Chase	Sierra
Clay	Skylar
Destiny	Trace
Devin	Trinity
Genesis	Wyatt
Heaven	Xander
Jade	Xavier

Sandra

An informal derivative of a Alesandra, which is a derivative of Alexandra, which is a derivative of Alexander. If names are onions, Sandra is the skin.[1]

Sarah

A name that requires no lips or teeth to pronounce. This is an excellent choice if you think your child might not be very smart. Having so simple a name just might keep her clear of stigmatizing speech therapy classes.

Sasha

For a brief time in the nineties we were allowed to like Russians, and that's when this pet name really caught on. Now we're not supposed to like them again, so if you see a Sasha, be mean to her.

Savannah

A nod to the great treeless plains. Most girls named Savannah turn out to be flat-chested.

Selena

Mexico's patron saint of popular music. The wound is so fresh that many people, upon hearing your baby's name,

---

1. But not the part of the onion one would throw into the trash.

will burst into tears and become inconsolable until you agree to change the baby's name.

Shana/Shayna/Sheena

If you happened to have conceived your baby while on an African safari, or if you soon will be visiting the Amazonian jungle and would like your daughter to fit right in, this one's for you. Sixty percent of all girls who grow up to marry monkeys bear one of these names.

Shania

This name don't impress me much. In fact, the name is a butchering of the Yiddish word for pretty, "shaina." Roughly translated, Shania might mean "not pretty." Probably it would just sound like nonsense.

Sharon

Although the American pronunciation of this name tends to sound more like "sharin'," Sharons are notoriously selfish girls.

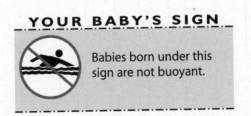

YOUR BABY'S SIGN

Babies born under this sign are not buoyant.

Sheila

In Australia, one can refer to any woman at all by the term "Sheila." A mother has to remove originality and distinctiveness from her criteria to choose this name.

Shelby

A big, clumsy, floppy-eared, Southern-sounding name. Even horses named Shelby seem resentful and sullen. Think of it this way: you have two dogs, one a Saint Bernard and one a Chihuahua. Which would you name Shelby?

Shelly

More often a derivative of Sheldon than of Michelle, this name is often mistaken for the adjective "shelly," a modifier indicating a particularly fishy scent.

Sherry

Un grand faux pas du mot français chéri.

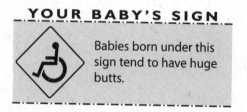

YOUR BABY'S SIGN

Babies born under this sign tend to have huge butts.

Shirley

When looking for a Shirley, one need only check beneath the huge hairdryers at a beauty parlor.

Sierra

The word *sierra* actually comes from the Latin *serra*, meaning "saw," as in the teeth of a saw. In nature, it refers to mountain ranges with ridges whose irregular shape reminds one of saw teeth. It also refers to fish. Large fish. Beautiful, huh?

Simonne

Ze Frenchest of zee French names for zee little beauty. She is beautiful, *non*? *Oui!* She wears a beret and hangs from her lovely mouth a cigarette—eet is sensuous, *non*?

Skye

A name that smells like patchouli and incense, babies named Skye feel most comfortable in tie-dye diapers.

Skylar

When girls named Skye grow up, they like to redefine themselves with this seemingly respectable derivative. Unfortunately, they remain as unconvincing as a pony-tailed hippie in a business suit.

Sophia

The ancient Greeks described one who had the ability to convince people of something regardless of its truth as a Sophist. Sophias carry on this trait as constant fibbers, forging notes from parents, stealing candy from their friends, and generally behaving in an untrustworthy manner.

Stacy

A little girl's name that can never be taken seriously on a corporate letterhead. In order to compensate for this phenomenon, most Stacys assume foul tempers and nasty dispositions.

Stephanie

Yet another derivative of a male name. Now is a good time to ponder if there are any male names that are derivatives of female names.

Summer

Everybody likes Summer. Summer's hot. Everyone can agree on that. Some people like to have Summer all year long. Some people have Summer up North, but others prefer a hot Summer in the South. Either way, everyone likes at least something about Summer.[1]

---

1. Although it is not specified here, this joke can easily turn very dirty.

Susan

The McDonald's of girls' names. There's one on every corner, and you know exactly what you're going to get when you get there. You don't question how they got there or even if it's a good idea to have so many; in fact, usually you don't even notice them.

Suzanne

A good way to best a neighbor who has named his daughter Susan. A lot like buying a luxury edition to best a neighbor's base model car: it looks a lot stronger and shinier, but in the end it's just a dressed-up version of the same old thing. Having to write the additional two letters every day isn't really worth it.

Sydney

A name better suited for your ninety-year-old uncle than your daughter. However, many families have gone with this choice in recent years, hoping to surprise the neighbors with their version of an original name idea: using old men's names for baby girls. Often this plan backfires when little Sydneys take to smoking cigars and ordering corned beef sandwiches at the Chuck E. Cheese. Most parents eventually reconsider this choice when their daughter is kicked out of daycare for continually patting the teacher on the ass and calling her "sweetie."

Tabitha

An undeniably perfect baby name. So good, in fact, that most Tabithas never manage to adjust to adulthood and wear diapers well into their forties.

Tamara

Many Tamaras go years without friends, since when Tamaras are asked their name, people feel brushed off by their response.

Tammy

A derivative without an original form. In recent years, scientists and historians have worked together to determine a possible forbearer for Tammy. Presently, they are leaning toward the now-extinct Tamothra, Tamborine, and Gotammit.

Tanya

The female version of Tonya, this name is often reserved for the prettier of twin girls. As such they become hated by their sisters, who eventually try to even the score by hiring guys to break their legs.

Tara

Either from the word meaning "hill" in Gaelic or just a suffix that somebody once mistook for a name. In either case, most kids feel gypped out when they find they got this name instead of a real one with lots of letters and stuff.

Tatiana

A name that actually comes with a crown and a letter declaring the baby in possession of the greatest syllable-to-letter ratio of any name in history. This is small compensation for a little girl who will grow up in constant shame of an unnecessarily extravagant name that sounds a little too much like "titty."

Taylor

Never has there been a time or place when working as a tailor or spelling it incorrectly was a sign of honor.

Teresa

Many Teresas, shamed by the piety of their namesake Mother Teresa, will ask others to refer to them as Terry. From there, the identity crises never end. Failed relationships follow, one after the other, until eventually Terry becomes Terrance and you are stuck with a wide-hipped son with a high voice and an addiction to testosterone supplements.

Tia

"Tia yellow ribbon round the old oak tree!" Tia is actually the first three letters of some other name that's never been identified. Bearers of this name tend to have trouble finishing their thoughts and often end up at the grocery store, late at night, unsure why they came.

Tierra

A gross misspelling of "tiara." For those who feel their little princess is destined for greatness, but only within the confines of the trailer park.

Tiffany

In medieval times, this name was given to girls born to the righteous during the Feast of the Epiphany. In present day, this name is given to girls who are born to the vacuous during the final round of *American Idol*.

YOUR BABY'S SIGN

Babies born under this sign will enjoy elevator sex when they grow up.

Tina

Four letters that have wandered off the end of Christina and Martina. Like Christmas without Christ; like Thanksgiving without the thanks; like Passover without the pass; like Ramadan without the ram; like Hanukkah without the hanuk.

Toni

For parents who'll be paying for their daughter's name, Toni provides an acceptable low-cost option to Antonia.

Tonya

The male form of the female name Tanya. This name is generally reserved for the less attractive of twin girls. Angered at their fate as second stringers in the beauty department, Tonyas tend to lash out at anyone prettier or more successful—even going so far as to hire people to break the legs of prettier girls.

Tori

From the Latin, meaning "bulging" or "swelling." The only time this name is appropriate and inoffensive for a girl is when she is pregnant, hence a disproportionate number of Toris can be found among the ranks of teenage pregnancies.

Tracy

From the French *tracier*, meaning "to trace," a word that first appeared in the eighteenth century, when girls were allowed to attend French schools. To identify cheaters, girls who were caught copying the work of the more intelligent boys were called Traci, "one who traces." Twentieth-century girls named Tracy often cut corners looking for an easy way to make a quick buck.

Trisha

Half a name. Girls named Trisha tend to spend long, depressing years in dead-end relationships, all the while claiming they are in search of someone to complete them.

Tyra

Sounds like an outburst shouted by a Libyan with Tourette's syndrome. "TYRA!"

Ula/Uma/Una

These are not actual names, but rather the utterances of people suffering from intestinal disturbances.

Valerie

From the Latin *valere*, "to be strong." Valeries tend to be men among women, playing softball, bowling, and sporting flannel shirts and mullets.

Vanessa

Greek for "butterfly," most girls named Vanessa spend long, awkward years eating leaves, uncomfortable with their own bodies. After a period of quiet reflection, Vanessas will then take on a new persona, dazzling friends and relatives with their newfound brilliance. Eventually Vanessas get caught, and they are pinned to a book, literally.

Veronica

Veronica, or "true image," refers to the facial image left on a hankie offered to Jesus by a woman named, surprisingly enough, Veronica. Girls named Veronica, entranced by the tale, tend to appreciate the facial particulars of Jesus manifested in their own faces, and thus never wax or pluck. This name is only recommended for fair-haired babies.

Victoria

Namesake of England's queen, who in the nineteenth century carved up India and Africa, redefining the scope of the term "imperialism" and spurring a global resentment toward the West that continues to plague the world today.

Virginia

Wishful thinking. So what are you going to call her when she's twenty-one? Sexuallyactivia?

Wendy

A cutesy best friend sort of name that guarantees lots of male friends, but never a boyfriend. This phenomenon was explored in *Peter Pan* when Wendy refuses to accept her role as Peter's best friend (the other Lost Boys actually referred to Wendy as Peter's "fag hag") and tries to . . . uh, convert him.

Winona

Sioux for "eldest daughter." Girls who are not, in fact, eldest daughters, yet are named Winona regardless, often disappear when angered Indian spirits haunt their houses and suck them into the TV.

Zoe

One of those names that feels stylish to some simply because no one they know is named Zoe. Of course, an AMC Pacer might, because of its distinctiveness, feel stylish too, but there is probably another reason you don't know anyone who owns one. They're ugly!

Boys' Names

Aaron

So you were hoping for a girl, huh? Your baby's namesake (or *Risky Biblical Business*): Moses's little brother, Aaron, might mean "house party" in ancient Hebrew. When Moses goes up on Mount Sinai for a few days, Aaron, a fast talker and a real crowd-pleaser, placates the mob by helping them trash the place.

Abraham

"Father of Nations." A hilarious name for those Abrahams who as adults find themselves infertile or impotent.

Adam

No one gives a dam about this name. According to the Bible, Adam was the first man. Later God got better at it. This is a popular name for parents who see their first son as a kind of work in progress.

Aden

A cheap attempt at getting your kid to the front of every line. If you're going to do this, you might as well call him AAA.

Adolf

A terrific name for those who are delighted to find their newborn baby already sporting a skinhead.

Adrian

Most famously Rocky's wife who stands beside him through even his most difficult challenges. Indicating loyalty and honor, a perfect name for your little girl . . . wait, for a boy? Ha, ha, ha, ha, ha, ha, ha (deep breath) ha, ha, ha, ha, ha!

Alan

Far more often employed as an acronym than anything else. As such, young Alans often find themselves learning of organizations that bear their name—most often these organizations don't make little Alans feel good about their chances.

Albert

Some parents believe that adding the prefix "Al" somehow denerdifies the name "Bert." It doesn't.

Alexander

History's most celebrated egomaniac. Widely credited with uniting most of his known world with his Grecian formula of Me + You = More Me, Alexander was tutored by some of the greatest thinkers in history, but he still turned out to be a fascist. Most boys named Alexander claim to be captain of their soccer teams—their teammates don't usually agree.

Alfred

Most strongly associated with Batman's doddering butler, a man who was wise to every one of Batman's secrets yet was only trusted to wash the costumes and answer the phone.

Ali

Most babies named Ali both float like butterflies and sting like bees. They often find themselves in trouble in daycare for executing rope-a-dopes.

Allen

A misspelling of the name Alan. Such children ordinarily end up in speech therapy sessions developed specifically for people who can't manage to acknowledge the commonly accepted pronunciations of such words as *ball*, *call*, and *fall*.

A

Amos

A holdover from those wacky days before the civil rights era.

Andre

Ooo la la! How very French of you! (translate into French) This name is most often chosen by African American families since white boys usually can't stand the beatings.

Andrew

Greek for "manly," this name is especially popular among poorly endowed fathers who fear that their sons might be lacking a bit in the masculinity department.

Angel

The perfect name for parents expecting to give birth to a feline. Most boys named Angel tend to fastidiously tidy and wash themselves with their tongues.

Angelo

Here's a funny one: Tell him he's actually your fifteenth kid, and you named the previous fourteen Angela, Angelb, Angelc, and so on. Hilarious, huh?

Anthony

A name of the great Italian tradition that brings to mind all the stereotypical associations one might have with people of Italian heritage: the mafia, the mob, gangsters, *The Godfather* . . . and Prince Spaghetti Day.

Ariel

Why, the most famous little mermaid of all! Just think how delighted your little princess—I mean prince—will be when he hears his name on the TV speaker at daycare. If he's lucky, the other kids'll give him the nickname "Little Mermaid." Maybe he'll even wear a Little Mermaid costume for Halloween!

Armando

Armando has a mustache and dark black hair. Armando is a lover. Armando goes to the European disco and parks his Toyota far from the view of the beautiful ladies who smell Armando long before he arrives. He is smooth, he is slick—he is a lover, this Armando.

Arthur

A real bow-tie, kick-your-ass-at-recess kind of name. To avoid such associations and somewhat denerdify the name, Arthurs often call themselves Art. They soon find, though, that they are unsuccessful.

Asher

A beautiful name from the Bible that has since been used as the lead character in Pokémon. Now, if you don't know what Pokémon is, this is probably your first kid. But take it from me, you don't want to name your kid after a cartoon character—it tends to strip a lot of dignity from the whole process.

Ashton

Man, you want to name your kid Ashton? You got punk'd!!!

Aubry

Here's a name that walks the razor wire of gender identity and poor spelling.

Austin

"The Father of Texas," Stephen Austin was actually from Missouri and only lived in the "big hat state" for fifteen years. While he was there, though, he bravely sent out infantry to kill as many Native Americans as they could find. Good old Austin managed to virtually wipe out the Indians and scare away the Mexicans so that when he was ready to die, Stephen Austin had made the great state of Texas safe for peace loving Anglo-Americans for years to come. A real American hero. Hee haw!

Avery

The problem with naming your son what was formerly only a surname is that as far as gender goes things are still being sorted out. Avery seems to be appropriate for both boys and girls. Most likely, this is because Avery isn't a first name.

Axel

More of a bar on which tires spin than a baby name, but I suppose if you are a car or skating enthusiast, this is a terrific name. Just be aware that most kids named Axel are assumed to be violently insane until they prove themselves otherwise. There's really no good reason for this, but it's generally true.

Barry

An androgynous sort of name. Other androgynous things that ought to come to mind before settling on Barry include rollerblades, jumpsuits, and David Bowie.

Beau

French for "handsome," most Beaus tend to be ugly and lonely, sitting home nights reflecting on the irony of their first name.

Benjamin

Ancient Hebrew for "son of the right hand," which cannot help but make us wonder how that's possible. Apparently, children named Benjamin join blindness and hairy palms as the consequences of using the right hand.

Bill/Billy

Kind of a pug-nosed, buck-toothed, freckly sort of name, Billys tend to wear checkered shirts and receive mediocre grades in school.

Blaire

A verb, meaning "to sound deafeningly." Listen to your kid cry. Feel like he's got a good set of lungs? Then go ahead, tag him!

Blake

Once the surname of a virtuous thinker and poet, now the name of thousands of suburban brats who are watering this name down worse than a martini at a retirement home.

Bob

So utterly boring, Bob looks the same forwards or back-wards, sliced in half and folded over itself, exhaled and inhaled. Interesting nature fact: Bob is the only name that frogs can say.

Brad

The smallest of all nails. So small that it can only be purchased in the hardware store's staple section. An excellent choice for poorly endowed boys.

Braedon

An Old English term that loosely translated means "Eyebrow Town." The term originates from a fifteenth-century Scottish amusement park divided into fun-filled towns celebrating underappreciated body parts. Eyebrow Town had a log ride and kind of a lame roller coaster made from chain mail and mud.

Brady

Not a name, but rather an adjective describing the condition of appearing Brad-like or behaving in a Brad-like manner. For instance, upon being asked out to attend an ornithology lecture by a boy in a bow tie, a girl might declare, "That guy is so *Brady*." In this case, the adjective is not complimentary.

Brandon

Brandon is generally chosen by families that plan to spoil their son to the extent that he will be rude and horribly disliked. Poor families do not choose this name since they are unable to fulfill their obligations in this regard.

Braxton

A surname held by residents of medieval towns wherein bricks would be produced. Upon leaving such towns, many residents were happy to discard the names, as they didn't really carry the prestige they had hoped they would.

Brayden

A Middle English term that referred to the room in the valley in which misbehaving children were kept—loosely translates as "the crying valley." Parents who plan on years of strict discipline tend to choose this name.

Brendan

A favorite among many pacifist parents who are unaware that they are naming their son after a weapon.

Brennan

A surname posing as a first name—a fairly recent trend of misnaming which seems to be applied only to the most spoiled and mean-spirited of children.

Brent/Brett

From the French word to describe a resident of Brittany. Most Bretts and Brents don't know this though and live most of their lives under the misconception that they have been named after some local newscaster with whom their mother shared a scandalous tryst.

Brian

Many dyslexic parents generally choose this name when actually hoping to name their son Brain.

Brock

Asher's libidinous sidekick on Pokémon. Most boys named Brock go on to anchor local news broadcasts, and most of the rest enjoy long tenures on daytime soaps. Fascinating fact: No one named Brock has ever had a bad hair day.

Brody

Hero of the aborted Saturday morning cartoon *Brody the Roadie*. A terrific kids' show about life on the road with a hard rockin', hard partyin' band and its many criminal and sexual misadventures. The show was taken off the air after a single episode. The name lives on.

Bruce

No one knows how this name turned into a sissy name, but it did. There's no denying it. Parents are betting their baby's dignity and potential masculinity when they write "Bruce" on the dotted line. And the payoff? Well, you get to call your kid Bruce. Not a very even benefit-risk ratio.

Bryce

One of the original genetic experiments designed to provide two of the basic food groups in a single item. Strands of broccoli DNA were combined with strands of rice DNA to create Bryce. The result was a race of pretentious, little suburban boys who smelled bad when boiled.

Bryson

The son of Brian. Ah, Brian: a name shared by no pope or president, the name of a man with nothing at all by which to remember his feeble existence other than his heirs. This is his son, the bearer of his hollow legacy—Bryson.

Caden

A Middle English term that refers to a kid that was abandoned by his mother. Such children tend to be paranoid and resentful . . . and their mothers are just jerks.

Caleb

Means "dog" in Hebrew. As such, it is a terrific choice for a dog's name. As a person's name, it does have certain disadvantages, chief among them being that it means "dog."

Calvin

The name of the original "work ethic" king! Boys named Calvin tend to buy into this myth until much later in life, when a string of failures forces a deep disillusion which eventually leads to nihilism, homelessness, and eventually death.

Cameron/Cam

A Gaelic nickname for people with crooked noses. Upon learning this fact, parents—afraid of what embarrassment may result from this oversight—often punch their babies in the nose. From that point on, these babies are called "Wards of the State."

Carl

Kind of a clumsy, clunky name. Boys named Carl tend to have big feet and floppy ears, and are often mistaken for stuffed animals. Hence, many Carls go missing when they are accidentally tossed in their grade school's Lost and Found.

YOUR BABY'S SIGN

Babies born under this sign will never be cool. Aaaaay!

Carson

(Holding an envelope against my forehead . . .) The children of automobiles, former talk show host, and absurdly serious name for boys who will develop Oedipal complexes for their family Chevy. (Opening the envelope and reading the enclosed index card. . . .) What is Carson.

Carter

One who carts. In the Middle Ages, when this name originated to identify those who carted, a Carter would cart such items as fruit, vegetables, garbage, mud, and bodies. Apparently, the most important qualification for pursuing a career in carting was the possession of a cart. Not much else. Over the centuries, a bit of the prestige and panache of this name has faded.

Casey

Originally sanctioned by the Rock Island Line Train Company as generic greeting for all of their conductors whose real names they had no interest in knowing.

Chad

Parents who name their children Chad know that they are flying in the face of common wisdom, as anyone who's watched a sitcom knows that Chads are wealthy jerks.

Chance

Well, you're rolling the dice with this name. A popular name in Vegas.

Chandler

Yeah, *Friends* was a terrific show. But now it's over. And all over America are little Chandlers, none of whom are quite as clever or cute as Matthew Perry.

Charles

It's feast or famine with Charles. Either you assume the pompous formality of Charles or you are left with the dopey Charlie, the beer-slamming Chuck, or jazzy Chaz. Fortunately, every day brings us closer to the legitimization of C-dog.

Charlie

Charles's dopey twin brother, Charlies tend to do poorly in school simply because whenever they do good work, their teachers assume they copied it.

Chaz

Most boys named Chaz tend to have trouble making it to their tables in the lunchroom without getting tripped along the way to the call of "Spaz!" Many young men choose to go by this variant of Charles, hoping to add a spark to their stodgy image. Instead, people just assume they're gay.

Christian

A Buddhist would not name his son Buddhist; a Hindu would not name his son Hindu. Ridiculous, right? That's how the name Christian sounds to the rest of the world. (Especially troublesome when combined with the middle name Scientist.)

Christopher

Hardly anyone goes by the formal name Christopher, mostly because it sounds so unmasculine. Instead, most young men adopt the name Chris, hoping for a big dose of testosterone. Since that just hasn't been the case, people have recently begun using Toph or Topher, preferring an unquestionably ugly name to a feminine one.

Clarence

That dopey angel who fell to Earth and put Jimmy Stewart through hell just to make a point he *could* have made in a short conversation.

Clay

Men named Clay tend to be easily manipulated, especially if you heat them up a bit.

Names That Remind People of Clay

Now I'm not talking about multicolored (and strangely appetizing) Play-Doh. I'm talking about the gray, formless, gob of mess piled on a potter's wheel in Art class. The kind of stuff that resembles nothing but clay, and even when spun, shaped, and glazed, still looks like a big mess.

Definitely some babies come out looking no better than this. But tossing a heavy, permanent clump of name on their heads doesn't help much. Babies with these names don't stand much of a chance of being very dynamic, dashing, fascinating . . . or even interesting people:

Bob	Henry
Brian	Joe
Bruce	Karla
Carol	Monica
Claudia	Tom
Clay	Oscar
Colby	Pamela
Cole	Shelby
Ellen	Warren
Frank	

Clayton

Means "clay town." Understand? Clay town. A town where clay is apparently in large supply. At least twenty-two towns in America are called Clayton . . . and now your son?

Clifford

You know why they chose this name for the big, dumb dog? Because it's a big, dumb name.

Clinton

Hey, I voted for the guy twice. But even I have to admit that this name's been stained worse than a blue party dress.

Cody

A perfect name for when your baby is born part dog and part cowboy.

Colby

After a big surge a couple of years ago, this name seems to be losing ground to other names in honor of our great cheeses. Names like Mozzarella for girls and the playful Cheddar for boys.

Cole

A big, round name for a big, round boy! Oh, ho ho ho!

Colin

In case naming your child Colin isn't humiliation enough, you might want to consider Anis, Rectim, or Biwel Mivement.

Colton

Means "coal town." Understand? Coal town. A town in which coal is apparently in large supply. At least five towns in America are called Colton . . . and now your son.

Connor

One who cons. One who lies with the hope of financial gain. A popular choice of those without high expectations for the moral rectitude of their sons.

Corey

While fifteen years ago this name was most associated with the twenty-three Hollywood actors who bore the name, now it is mostly associated with petty theft, drug use, and *E! Hollywood Stories*.

Craig

A Gaelic term referring to the craggy hills and the craggy people who would occasionally wander down from them.

Curtis

Sometime during the seventies when the name Kurt was becoming popular, it was decided that a name was needed to identify the more effeminate Kurts. This is the result of that period's ugly gender warfare.

Dakota

The history of the Dakota goes like this: Originally, they were a tribe in pre-colonial America. Then they were expelled from their land and systematically exterminated by Europeans. Later, the great-great-grandchildren of these Europeans named their cars, their dogs, and eventually their children Dakota because they liked the earthy sound of it.

Dallas

Loosely translated, this name means "place in which one rests" (i.e., a rest room!). A rest room. I suppose there are worse places you could name your son after, but none really come to mind right now.

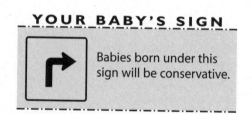

YOUR BABY'S SIGN

Babies born under this sign will be conservative.

Dalton

An atomic mass unit equal to one-twelfth of the atomic mass of 12C. As in, "The ants grew larger than buildings after we accidentally poured 2500 daltons of deadly uranium into their holes."

Damian

Do you think it simply coincidental that the name of the child in *The Omen* and the priest in *The Exorcist* are both Damian? While you may not be evil yourself, you can be sure that everyone who knows you will think you are. And your kid? He'll hate your guts. And you'll shrink in embarrassment as he says so. Then again, you just might not notice since the minions of Satan doing his evil bidding can be rather distracting.

Damon

Damon is the name of a Pythagorean who lived 2500 years ago. Do you know what a Pythagorean is? These are guys who devoted themselves to a philosophy based on math, and consequently lived like mathematicians. That is, boringly. Oh yeah, and they felt that beans were evil. Seriously. Pythagoreans briefly ruled Greece until people got so ticked off that they executed the whole lot of them. Then they tossed their dead bodies into a bean field.

Dane

Here's the question you have to ask yourself: Are you going to get bent out of shape when his coach refers to him as "Great Dane"? Are you going to get mad when he asks to have that put on the back of his soccer jersey? No? You're lying.

Daniel

A name made famous by the biblical Daniel, "psychic friend" and the world's first lion tamer. Out of respect for its religious nature, many parents have not allowed the name Dan or Danny to be lettered onto the back of their son's soccer jersey. Hence, Daniels tend to be hated by their teammates and coaches, who are constantly being corrected for calling them "Danny."

Dante

The Italian poet Dante is most famous for having written an account of hell that has managed to frighten the hell out of a lot of people.
You should read this to your son when he is little—he'll get a kick out of knowing about another Dante. Plus, he'll never sin.

Darius

Name of the ancient Persian king who is noted in the New Testament as *not* wanting to kill all the Jews in his country. I don't know. I think that's setting a pretty low bar.

Darren

Samantha's gangly, dopey husband who spent years trying to repress his wife's natural inclination to practice witch-craft. Now your wife is a witch. Think how cool that is! And this dope won't let her cast any spells? What's the matter with this jerk? Anyway . . . hmmm . . . what were we talking about? Oh, Darren. The biggest problem with this name is situational. When your son gets married and his wife introduces him at crowded parties she will proba-bly say, "I'm so-and-so, and my husband's Darren," which because of the noise they'll hear as ". . . and my husband's barren." And that's just nobody's business.

David

The shepherd King David is responsible for so many psalms that one cannot help but describe him as one of the first and most appreciated poets. It is a line of poetic and liter-ary genius that stretches from four thousand years ago to the writing of this book, *The Worst Baby Name Book Ever*, by David Narter. David, a name of unparalleled promise.

Names That Animals Are Likely to Telepathically Whisper to Crazy People

It's not very likely that anyone who buys this book is going to hear the demonic murmurs of stray dogs . . . but you never know. Take it from me. Hearing your name being soundlessly uttered from every damned dog you pass on the sidewalk can be a pretty maddening experience. Really maddening. It also doesn't leave much room for the other voices in my head.

I know that were I naming a child, I would want to decrease the likelihood of him or her having to deal with this entirely avoidable problem as much as possible. For sane children, consider striking the following from your list:

David	David	David
David	David	David
David	David	David
David	David	David
David	David	David
David	David	David
David	David	David
David	David	David
David	David	David
David	David	David
David	David	David
David	David	David

Davis

The surname of the president of the Confederacy, a man who did everything he could to destroy this country in his time.

Dawson

Son of Daw. Now, Daw isn't actually a name, but some historians believe Daw means "David." In certain tribes of poor enunciators Daw, in fact, might have passed for David, but those tribes are long since extinct as they often found themselves in battles with other tribes who found their way of talking worthy of ridicule, hysterical laughter, and brutal evening ambushes.

Dax

Not so much a name as an odd collection of letters that together make a sound similar to that made by a dog clearing its throat.

Declan

The problem here is that due to relative rarity of the name, people unfamiliar with it will read it as D-clan, which doesn't sound nearly as cool as Declan. Another problem when pronounced incorrectly is that it sounds like you might have named him as a tribute to the KKK.

D

Demetrius

Nine letters? Nine letters and not a chance of shortening it? Give the kid a break—he's going to get writer's cramp in kindergarten.

Dennis

Ah, the menace. Why is it so difficult to imagine this name attached to anyone with dark hair . . . or older than twelve? Sometimes people grow and their names just can't keep up. As adults, many Dennises shed this name and go by the name Harvey. That might explain why there are not many adults named Dennis and even fewer children named Harvey.

Denver

In one of history's great ironies, James Denver, whose last name means "ferry of the valley," founds the Mile High City! With a nod to this paradox, most parents of Denvers plan to raise their boys as girls.

Denzel

Sounds a lot more like a pharmaceutical product than a name. But who knows? Maybe there's some patent money to be made here.

Derek

If Derek weren't a name, it would be a power tool.

Babies born under this sign think it's funny to urinate in public.

Desmond

So many families are choosing this name in honor of Bishop Desmond Tutu of South Africa. But nobody chooses Tutu! What's the problem with Tutu?

Devin

Isn't it funny how original people think they're being by changing a single letter in a common name from *K* to *D*? Maybe you should consider something *really* crazy. How about instead of dressing him in blue, you dress him green?!? Isn't that outrageous?

Devon

I suppose if you're going to name your kid after a city, you could do a lot worse. As opposed to little Houston (250 murders per year) or little Dallas (200 per year), little Devon will be representing a city with only four or five killings per year. Of course, he won't have much "street cred."

Dexter

Years ago, Professor Dexter Hildensour ran several studies to determine why parents choose the name Dexter when they can be sure that they are virtually guaranteeing an unhappy childhood for their son. Dr. Hildensour found that these parents were suffering from a condition he identified as "idiocy." The term he devised to refer to such people was "idiots." As yet, no one has developed a cure for this unfortunate condition, but scientists work round the clock in the hope that someday "idiocy" will be eradicated—and all children will be safe.

Dick

Oh, the magic of Dick. He'll hate you for life, but never you mind. You stick with Dick. You hold Dick tightly and never let go. The last major public official to actually stick with this name was Richard Nixon—and he was a real Dick. A Dick that was bigger than life. Now, your parents are going to accuse you of shoving Dick down their throats, but don't you believe it. Most people that claim to dislike Dick, deep down really don't. So don't be afraid of Dick. It's what everybody secretly wants, and you can have it. Raise your Dick proudly and say to the world, "I don't care what you think, world! I love Dick!!!"

Dirk

Odd but true: To Dirk someone is to stab them with a knife. Usually a Dirk knife.

Dominic

Although the root of the name indicates the common translation of "belonging to the lord," many modern scholars believe that Dominic can roughly be translated into a Greek expression for "Pete's brother."

Donald

Oh, such hilarious icons are presently associated with this name—some timeless, some brainless. First, of course, that lovable, pantsless, rage-aholic duck. Then, the classically coiffed megalomaniac who could buy and sell this book (well, really anyone could). And let's not forget that cranky fella who's always siccing the FBI on me. That's quite a brood. But they just might have room for one more. . . .

Donovan

You can name him Donovan if you like; regardless, they'll call him Mellow Yellow. Quite rightly.

Dorian

What are you going to call him for short? Dor? That's a thing. Dori? That's a girl's name. Save yourself the aggravation and just have a girl.

Doug

You can always count on a guy named Doug . . . to bore you to death. He'll be the only kid in first grade to declare his ambition to sell life insurance.

Drake

The greatest of English explorers, Sir Francis Drake plundered the Spanish ports in Brazil and Peru, and stole all their maps. When he ran out of maps to steal, he stole their navigators. He was eventually knighted as England's greatest thief . . . oops! . . . explorer. The name also refers to a male duck—apparently a far more honorable designation.

Drew

The past tense of draw. Drew is also the latter half of the name Andrew. As such, Drews tend to feel incomplete, as if they were part of something larger that they just can't identify. As a result, disproportionate numbers of Drews populate American cults.

Dustin

A misspelled participle referring to the act of spreading fine particles over a large space, or the removal of said particles by means of a feather duster.

Dylan

A rebellious and poetic name that seems to have lost a lot of its beauty and edginess since the U.S. Census recently found that all minivans, at some time, will transport a Dylan to a soccer game.

Earl

Very few names are actually derived from medieval positions of royalty. Perhaps that's because the very idea of praising royalty for royalty's sake is offensive to any decent citizen.

Edward

This is the sort of name that fits best on the nameplate of a stone-faced bank executive. If names were facial expressions, Edward would be a frown.

Elijah

The first of the major prophets to let us know that we are all going to suffer a horrible apocalypse one day. Ever wonder why you never heard the nickname "Goodtime Elijah"? Probably because no one has ever had it!

Elliot

Ouch. ET's little friend and the last six letters of the word Smelliot. Fortunately most kids won't be clever enough to come up with that one, so they'll just call him Idiot. It's not terrifically clever, but fourth-grade bullies have never prided themselves on cleverness, only an ability to wound without remorse.

Emiliano

Here's an interesting origin. A guy named Emil moves into town and all the girls fall for him. So another guy decides to one-up him and calls himself Emila and his wife Emilia. But then another guy shows up and outdoes them all with Emiliano! Years from now, your kid'll get bested by some guy named Emilianopoly.

Emmanuel

Meaning "God is with us." In biblical times, when miracles like parting the sea and raising the dead were performed, this name was commonly shouted in fear and paired with such expletives as Holy S**t!

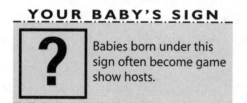

YOUR BABY'S SIGN

?

Babies born under this sign often become game show hosts.

Eric

Though no baby is born covered in freckles and orange hair, most named Eric eventually develop both as if they were victims of some Nordic disease of predestination. Someday a virus will be developed to end this horror, but until then the World Health Organization has advised parents to stay away from this name.

Ernest

Boys named Ernest are notoriously loud and dishonest. Boys who actually *are* earnest see the irony, but are too polite to point it out.

Ethan

Whereas this name used to have a revolutionary air to it, in recent years one most associates the name Ethan with suburban soccer games and shouts of "Kick the ball, Ethan!"

Eugene

Eugene, another victim of the dot-com boom and bust, has hung up its glasses and pocket protectors and been retired.

Evan

A name originating from medieval times when knaves would try to woo princesses, disguising their identities by means of cleverly transposing the letters in their titles. Those going by the name of Evan were the dumbest of these imposters but invariably the most successful, since those who transposed their names correctly as Evank were immediately caught.

Ezekiel

The strangest of all Bible stories, one in which people are smitten, brought to life, smitten again, and again brought to life. Ezekiel plays a big role in the whole thing . . . well, maybe not so big a role . . . actually he's just there.

Ezra

One of the Bible's most exotic names, in that way that "exotic" is sometimes synonymous with "really ugly."

Fabian

From the Latin *faba,* or "fava bean." Many parents are completely against naming their sons after legumes, but others recognize the threat that such vegetables pose to the human race and are positioning their sons to the front of the ranks when the revolution comes . . . that's the only explanation I can come up with. Why else would a person name his or her son after a bean?

Felix

America's two most famous Felixes are a fastidious and strangely effeminate divorcé, and a talking cat.

Forrest

American cinema's most famous mentally challenged hick. A strange choice for a name since the word really means "place with lots of trees."

Frank

Let me be Frank. A boy named Frank has to decide very early in his life if he will go with the old man name (Frank) or choose to be beat up daily for signing "Francis" to his schoolwork. Frankly, that's a difficult dilemma to force upon a kid. If I may be so Frank.

Fred

A name used exclusively to pay tribute to older and deader relatives named Fred.

Gabriel

A name inextricably tied to the act of tooting one's own horn. Perfect for babies that just blow.

Gage

When you throw a glove on the ground or slap another person in the face with it, you are offering a Gage. Babies named Gage tend to be overly confrontational and generally paranoid.

Garrett

Ancient Germanic name meaning "hard sword." Not only a terrific name for a baby but certain to be even more popular when it becomes the name of a new erectile dysfunction drug.

Gary

The origin of this name could be either Germanic, in which cases it means "spear," or Basque, in which case it means or "person who lives near a barn." In America, it generally means, "city where many are poor." Either way, the tradition behind Gary is not too spectacular.

George

Here's an idea. Take a vote amongst your relatives to determine what to call your baby. Make it a choice between George and—oh, I don't know—let's say, Al. Tally all the votes and no matter who wins just declare George the winner.

Gerald

Short for Geraldine,[1] which was Flip Wilson's real name.[2]

---

1. Not true.
2. Also, not true.

Gordon

A name that sounds terrific at first, but soon loses its luster as relatives insist on calling the baby Gordo.

Graham

For boys whose parents believe that their sons are special enough to enjoy the great honor of sharing a name with one of America's finest after-school snacks. Boys named Graham, if unable to fulfill their duties as such, must give up the name and agree to be called Ritz.

Grant

Generally people make friends with guys named Grant only because they're expecting something.

Grayson

Son of gray? Son of a color? And not even an interesting color?! Gray, second only to tan in color boredom. How about Purpleson? Or Burnt Siennason?

Greg

If Greg were not a name, it would be a verb that describes the act of forcing a small amount of food eaten an hour ago up from the back of the throat.

Griffin

The Griffin is a Greek mythological creature that had the head of an eagle and the body of a lion. As a tribute to the horrors of radiation on the unborn, the Griffin stands proudly. As a name for your child—well, I don't know, maybe if the kid's really scary-looking?

Harley

A great way to honor fat, hairy motorcycle riders. Most Harleys are born with a mullet.

Harold

Often awarded to a third or fourth child by parents who, after they've given out the good stuff, decide to experiment with a quirky clunker like Harold. Thus far, it hasn't worked out so well.

Harrison

Son of Harry. Not Harold, but Harry. As if your son's real father is an old fella in a recliner trying to read his evening paper over the constant chattering of his nosey wife, Gladys.

Hayden

The building on a farm in which the hay is kept. Originally the name chosen by farmers to name those children conceived in a barn.

Holden

So you're a little hopeless and cynical, huh? Good for you. And what a terrific way to introduce your kid into the world! Name him after American literature's most defeated and disillusioned boy. Nevertheless, we're all very impressed that you read a book.

Howard

A&E is hoping this name sticks around since they've recently discovered that 50 percent of their audience for *Murder She Wrote* and *Matlock* is named Howard.

Hugo

Isn't it weird how cool this name sounds after the name Victor and how lame it sounds by itself? Isn't that weird? In cartoons, Hugos tend to be both fat and nerdy—a lethal combination and a terrible precedent.

Hunter

A name that evokes all the romance of cold Saturday mornings knee-deep in frigid swamp water waiting for one of God's creatures of beauty to approach . . . so you can kill it.

Ian

This name dates back to the Irish Potato Famine, when families were often too poor to afford more than one consonant per child.

Isaac

One of more gullible characters of the Bible. Abraham convinces Isaac to come up a hill to sacrifice a lamb, and not until he is splayed out on a rock beneath the upstretched, knife-wielding hands of his father does Isaac figure out that *he* is the sacrifice. Zoinks! Later, when he's old and blind, Isaac is tricked by his wife into giving his blessing to the wrong kid. Isaacs have trouble getting regular work since they are usually the guys who open virus e-mails.

Isaiah

No matter how relaxed this kid gets, he'll still have to live up to this ultra-serious name, which originated from the most important prophet of the Bible. Like fitting your kid for concrete booties.

Israel

Listen, a country in the Middle East has this name tied up. If you want to fight them over it, you'll just have to get in line.

Ivan

OH, YES. IS GOOD, THIS NAME. WITH LARGE BOOTS AND BOOMING VOICE, IVAN WILL BE KNOWN. IS BIG, THIS IVAN. IN KINDERGARTEN, IS BOY WITH STRONG ARMS AND WODKA ON BREATH.

Jace

Not only a baby name, but also the newest craze in criminal friendly, 100 percent juice, theft deterrents. Tastes terrific and won't stain your clothes. So the next time she wants to give you a face full of mace, ask for a can of Jace.

Jack

A real trouble-maker. Jack has historically been a nickname of boys named John. Lately, apparently to have their sons taken less seriously, parents have been using Jack as a formal birth name. The effect has been difficult on hospitals, as babies who would otherwise take the business of being a baby seriously by crying, sleeping, and fussing have now taken to smoking in their cribs and engaging the other babies in three-pacifier Monty games.

Jackson

Son of Jack. Jack's son. A particularly confusing choice when made by the many parents who are not named Jack.

Jacob

Even God didn't like this name. He hated it so much that He just told the biblical Jacob that he couldn't use it anymore. Most kids named Jacob spend a lot of time looking at the sky, waiting for the other shoe to drop.

Jadon

This name will probably get popular when we start living on spaceships.

Jaiden/Jaden

This isn't really a name so much as a random collection of letters. It has no meaning and serves only to make Jaidens who frequent bars have to repeat their name so often that they immediately turn off the women they are hitting on. "No no! Not Jason! Jaiden! My name is Jaiden! J-A-I . . . oh, forget it."

Jake

Everybody's buddy! Jake is a pal! The sort of kid who'll open up your house when you're on vacation and have the wildest, kickin'-est party your town's ever seen. Way to go, Jake! You rock!

Jalen

Another "J" spaceman name. Someday, we will vacation on the moon and swim in the mighty oceans of Venus. In those days, Jalens will take us there in their silver space-ships as we ride out of the atmosphere and into the wide expanse of deepest space. Jalens tend to watch a lot of Sci-Fi channel.

Jamal

Yet another name that means handsome. Of course, there is no way a mother could ever know for sure that her son, at this point in his life, will be handsome. So she's either optimistic or just a big, fat liar. Most boys named Jamal describe their mothers as insincere.

James

The plural form of the name Jame. As such, most boys named James waste years of their lives in a futile search for their lost siblings.

Jason

Greek hero most noted for traveling far and wide in search of an attractive coat.

Javan/Javon

Odd, but true: A word that the countries of the East would use to refer to people from Greece during the time of Alexander the Greek. As in, "Those damn Javons invaded again!"

Jaxon

A horribly pretentious or grossly misspelled version of Jackson. Son of Jack. Now, if your name were Jack, this might make a little sense (although you'd selfishly be denying your son a name of his own). But Jaxon isn't even how you spell it! What's the matter with you?

Jay

More of a letter that nobody ever uses than a name.

Jaylon

A misspelling of Jalen. One of the sons of the biblical Ezra whose only distinguishing feature is that his name is mentioned last. That's about it.

Jeffrey

A freckly, big-eared, gangly sort of name—for parents that aren't expecting their baby to be particularly good-looking.

Jeremy

From the prophet Jeremiah, a worry wart in his own times. Jeremys tend to be the class narcs and are often incapacitated by atomic wedgies after predicting that everyone who's goofing off while the substitute teacher's in charge is going to "get it" when the teacher gets back. Many Jeremys find themselves teacher appointees to the student council. Though this launches the public service career of many a Jeremy, most of them can't manage to garner many votes. This would explain the disproportionately small number of Jeremys in the House of Representatives.

Jerome

A grave and heavy name, so depressing that even hyperactive kids can't find anything distracting about kids named Jerome. Babies named Jerome tend to be a drag. They are rarely invited to parties.

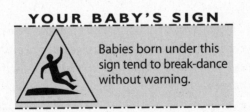

YOUR BABY'S SIGN

Babies born under this sign tend to break-dance without warning.

Jesse

Hee-haw! A name that just moseyed on straight from that there Bible into the Wild West and done rested right there in them there minivans. 'Bout as interesting as a cow in a stampede: probably thinking it's all purty and such, but you and I know ain't nothin' but another cow.

Jesus

Although you certainly see Jewish kids named Abraham or Moses, and Muslim kids named Mohammad, there remains a bit of sanity in the practice as the fellas in question were supposed to be mere prophets, not *God* himself. While some parents who've named their child Jesus may feel like they've done the kid a service, in reality it plays a lot like buying a Cadillac and driving through the neighborhood honking the horn, obnoxiously drawing attention to yourself.

Jim/Jimmy

When you name your kid an informal derivative of a formal name, you send all the wrong messages about propriety and decorum. Such boys spit indoors and talk loudly in movie theaters.

Joaquin

Nobody likes names with silent letters. It's pretentious and a real waste of time. Think of all the wasted labor every time someone needs to type *J* on a piece of mail, or every time your own little Joaquin has to write that extra silent letter on his homework. Think how confused he'll be in first grade when the teacher explains what sound the letter *J* makes, and he'll say, "What about the sound of nothing? Doesn't *J* also make no sound at all?" The teacher will roll her eyes and think, "What a ridiculous child."

Joe

While nobody finds this name particularly attractive, it has economic value in that plenty of bowling shirts and factory overalls have the name Joe already embroidered on them.

John

So common a name that even in the New Testament two different guys are named John.

Jonah

Biblical Jonah pissed off God so badly that He sent a whale to eat the guy.

Jonas

A female version of Jonah, based on the presumption that God was angrier at Jonah for cross-dressing than for not preaching in Nineveh.

Jordan

A popular name during the reign of Bulls star Michael Jordan. Now that he's retired, other NBA stars are getting their chance. You might want to consider these up-and-coming names for your boy: Garnett, Yow, or possibly Boozer.

Joseph

Of Biblical fame, Joseph was one of Jacob's many, many, many sons. Anyway, one day his brothers toss Joseph into a pit and sell him into slavery. Not one brother says that getting rid of Joseph was a bad idea. Not one! It was unanimous! Now, how good a guy could he have been?

Joshua

Kind of the General MacArthur and John Wayne of the Old Testament, responsible for more righteous slaying than the rest of the Bible's characters combined. Consider signing the birth certificate in blood.

Josiah

The female version of the girl's name Josie. A lot of parents think that, like double negatives, the "ie" and "ah" would cancel each other out, and the name would automatically become male. Unfortunately, that principle doesn't apply here.

Julian

From the Latin for "man who feels like man, but is wearing the clothes of a woman." Actually, that's not true. Still, this is one of the few names about which people might believe that.

Julius

A name less associated with its magisterial Roman past than with those frozen drinks they sell at shopping malls and county fairs.

Justice

Okay, fine. But don't blame me when he goes blind. You were asking for it. Seriously, what if he does go blind? Every time you have to explain that "Justice is blind," people are going to laugh. They won't want to, but they will.

J

Famous Dictators of the Detention Hall: A Timeline

Butch (194?–1962)

Led the Crewcut Armies of Eisenhowerburg to many victories over the Sputniks. Gum smacking, drawing on desks, stink bombs, and fart noises are all credited to this first and greatest leader.

Rocco (1962–1963)

The first in the line of Great Italian Tormentinis, Rocco invented the spitball. Tragically choked to death when his own straw backfired.

Vince (1963–1967)

Vinnie the Magnificient was known for his elaborate hairstyles. Unfortunately, Vince was later discovered to have suffered major brain hemorrhages as a result of the chemical reaction caused by large amounts of Dep entering his system by way of overloaded hair follicles.

Frank (1968–1972)

Revolutionized the wedgie by developing new techniques such as "the twist, "the clean jerk," and "the power wedgie." Statues of Frank the Wedgifier, as he came to be known, still adorn detention halls in each state in the union. His boldest political move came in 1969 when he rejected the annexing of the Hippie Freaks.

The Worst Baby Name Book Ever

Ralph (1972–1975)

Known affectionately as the Clown King. Ralph was unable to maintain control over the detention hall when the Nose Picking Scandal of 1975 brought his eventual downfall. Often credited with inventing the "noogie."

Damien (1975–198666)

The darkest days of the detention hall were ruled by Damien the Scary as Hell. Damien ruled longer than any other dictator, but all records of his dealings are written in ancient Aramaic and all attempted translations were aborted when the sky began raining blood.

Gerald (1986–1991)

Originally tossed into detention for taking football bets, Gerald the Boring revolutionized the hall by introducing computers to burnouts who promptly figured out how to use them to "score more weed, dude."

Nick (1991–1998)

Nick the Slacker, formerly of the Grunge Party, ruled reluctantly over the detention hall for most of the nineties but claimed to be doing so just because there wasn't anything else to do.

Rudy (1999–present)

It has been suggested that Rudy the Gameboy is not even aware that he's in detention, as most of his political objectives and attention seem focused on "getting to the next level."

Justin

Originally a derivation of the words *justice* and *just*, Justin has of late been a popular name among rapper daddies, who will often add an apostrophe to the end so that it becomes a verb—as in, "I been Justin' all day." Nobody is sure what that means, but some radio stations have reported that it's "chill" to be Justin'.

Kade

This name actually originated from a brainstorming session at Marvel Comics at which cartoonists were attempting to come up with a new superhero. While Kade, a lime-colored crime fighter, who maintains his superhuman strength with a diet of plenty of green, leafy vegetables and regular cardiovascular workouts, was eventually rejected, the name lives on.

Kai

More of an exclamation than a name. The sort of verbal nonsense someone with Tourette's syndrome might blurt out. "Kai!"

Kayden

Though this name has been growing in popularity in recent years, parents who choose it are frequently overwhelmed by friends and relatives who insist, "Kayden isn't a name!"

It's a bit like when cute little kids run the wrong way on a soccer field, despite the calls of their hysterical parents that they're "going the wrong way!" The kids just keep running down that field—sure of themselves and entirely ignorant.

Keaton

A last name that never really feels like a first name. Boys with such double-last names tend to drag behind on footraces, take too long to eat their supper, and always end up on teams that finish dead last.

Keegan

In Celtic (or Gaelic or whatever that language is), this name means "son of Egan." So as the son of Phil or Bruce, Keegan seems a little ridiculous. Odder still are the hundreds of female Keegans who are neither born to Egans nor are sons. Somewhere, there is a Keegan who is a vegan—and man, that dude is the butt of a lot of bad punch lines!

Keith

The name was first documented when in fifteenth-century Scotland a census registrar mistook the sound of a dog's sneeze as the name of one of the occupants of a house.

K

Kelly

A pathetic "Kiss me, I'm Irish" plea, this name is particularly sad when chosen by an obviously *non-Irish* couple.

Kelvin

Originated in 1936, when an illiterate dad with a speech impediment, intending to name his son Kevin, dictated his baby's name to the nurse filling out the birth certificate.

Ken/Kenneth

Most famously, Barbie's eunuchized boyfriend. If Ken were ever able to score, he might have a hard time convincing Barbie he's a male since the only difference between the two of them is his flat, muscular chest. If you've seen women bodybuilders, though, you know that Ken can't depend on his chest to justify his choice of gender. As the foremost representative of this name, Ken does not do a great job.

YOUR BABY'S SIGN

Babies born under this sign often grow up to be bullfighters.

Kendall

The perfect playground name, as it could be roughly translated to mean "King of the Mountain!" Even before they learn to speak, Kendalls are pushing the other daycare babies onto their diaper-cushioned butts and unintelligibly shouting and waving their arms victoriously.

Kennedy

Roughly translated from the Old Gaelic, this name means "ugly face." Actually a better translation would be "ugly head," but who cares? If your baby's ugly enough, people will know what you meant.

Kerry

Although it has been documented that Kerrys have long served in student council and even twice received Principal's Awards for breaking up playground fights, many students dispute the record, claiming that the Kerrys did not break up any fights. The Kerrys, for their parts, have long ago thrown the Awards into the trash in protest. A general consensus seems to be that the events in question took place in the second grade and should be left there.

Kevin

A fascinating statistic: 95 percent of all babies named Kevin are Irish. In explaining why this might be, sociologist Iwona Tinkle says, "It's because the name's so damned ugly! Who the hell else would want it?"

Kirk

Likely nickname: Kirk the Jerk. Not very popular until recently, mostly because the name sounds like a word you'd use to describe minor imperfections in your car's finish. The most famous Kirk is a libidinous spaceman who'd divert his ship's course for any sparkly, green tramp who floated past his monitor.

Kobe

Despite its popularity in the 1990s, I have a feeling this name won't be around much longer.

Kurt

A Middle English name that started in Germany and eventually spread to France and England. In Germany, Kurt was a surname that essentially meant "shorty." It can be assumed that few people would voluntarily name themselves and their progeny Shorty, so it can also be assumed that it's more of an insulting nickname than anything else. The French, always looking for a good insult, liked it so much they started calling the mini-French families Curt or Short Family. Eventually, people forgot what it meant and started calling their kids Curt and Kurt, just because they liked the name. Who knows? Maybe if you name your baby Kurt and he stays pretty short himself, you can have a good laugh about his name's ironic history.

Kyle/Kyler

A Kyler is one who Kyles. What "to kyle" means hasn't yet been specified in English. Assuming that Kyling might be a good thing . . . like feeding starving kids or building houses for the poor . . . to be a Kyler seems an honorable life. Of course, Kyling could refer to the act of spitting while riding a roller coaster, in which case, nobody's going to like your kid. To be honest, a kid that spits on rollercoasters isn't going to be popular no matter what his name.

Lance

A name that feels less at home on an American baby than on a young dragonslayer in an epic quest for the ancient stone of Zuwonder in the kingdom of Ziythuth.

YOUR BABY'S SIGN

Babies born under this sign will never need Viagra.

Landen

Kind of a pathetic thing really. This name found its way on to birth certificates by way of tribute to the actor and humanitarian Michael Landon. Of course, he spells his name differently. So it's only *kind of* a tribute. Kind of the way Kaitlyn is a tribute to Katelyn. Or the way Utah is a tribute to German singer Ute Lemper. Or the way Anfernee is a tribute to Anthony . . . oops, that just seems like a misspelling. Kind of like Landen.

Lane

Many people see a lane as only worthy of being walked upon, but in fact, Lanes can also be driven upon, skipped across, and spat upon.

Langdon

As if Landen was not a bad enough butchering of Landon. The first guy to request this on a birth certificate was shooting for Landon when he got part of a corned beef sandwich caught in his throat.

Lawrence

Children named Lawrence have a hopeless choice to make as they can go by either Lawrence or Larry, neither of which will make them any friends. Such children tend to grow pessimistic and depressed, eventually opting for a career in either proctology or podiatry.

Leonardo

No matter how handsome you think your little Leonardo is, you won't be able to convince anyone he's got anything on Leonardo DiCaprio. And they're probably right! I mean, how handsome can a drooling, bald sack of fat be?

Leslie

Some boys' names are also girls' names. Some other names are *just* girl names. From the time they are babies, Leslie boys are frequently mistaken for Leslie girls and given pink flowery jumpers as gifts. In first grade, they are encouraged to read *Babysitter Club* books and often are sent to the wrong bathroom. By adulthood, most Leslies just give in to the pressure and get the sex change. Others stick it out and live lives of intolerable sadness marked by gender confusion.

YOUR BABY'S SIGN

With the proper license, babies born under this sign may be stuffed and mounted.

Levi

Perhaps most popular in the late fifties though the eighties, few people bother with Levis anymore. These days they are more likely to prefer Calvin, Abercrombie, and Fitch.

Liam

An Irish name that might very well have been equivalent to Sam during a crisis of the sixteenth century, when peasant families couldn't afford the letter *s*.

Lloyd

A ridiculously spelled name, but perfect for the baby with three nipples.

Logan

A sleek spy name that sounds absolutely silly when referring to a drooling babbler. Logan is also one of those names that can't be turned into a nickname. Some fathers do call their sons Log, but they only do so when they are angry.

Lorenzo

As smooth and silky as Corinthian leather.

Louis

The name of sixteen French kings, most of which are remembered for being insensitive buffoons who brought about their own destructions. The last few Louises were so bad at being kings that after getting rid of them, France decided to do away with the whole idea of having kings at all.

Luca

When parents want to name their kid Luke or Lucas, but still want to feel as if they are entirely unique and hip, they go with Luca. Of course, it's a substitute name. It's not Luke. All Lucas are essentially "not Luke." As if they would have been Luke, had not a lot of other people thought of it first. It's like buying an off-brand at Aldi, like Captain Munch or Skeetles: not quite what you want, but it'll do.

Lucas

While many parents often mistake this for a name, it is actually a noun referring to the many copies of Suzanne Vega albums, called Lukas, that sit in remainder bins waiting for a return of the singer-songwriter era.

Luke

A very popular name among comic book collectors and sci-fi conventioneers. Apparently, many Lukes run away from home at sixteen citing frustration with what they call their "loser parents' obsession with teaching me to use the force." One more interesting fact: Babies named Luke tend to puke . . . . more often than other babies.

Mark

Nobody likes a Mark. As much as she'll say she loves him, leave a Mark on the dinner table and your mother will never forgive you. Even in school, everybody gets bad Marks now and then, and nobody's happy to have them. Good Marks are always a happy surprise, but hardly worth the trouble.

YOUR BABY'S SIGN

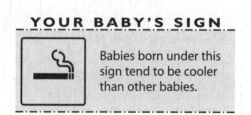

Babies born under this sign tend to be cooler than other babies.

Marshall

There is nothing funnier than a kid named Marshall that gets pushed around. Try this: name your kid Marshall and then raise him as a wimp. Keep him away from sports and build in him a love for opera and needlepoint. Then sit back and watch the merriment begin!

Martin

A name derived from Mars, Roman god of war and fertility. Hilariously, Martins are disproportionately less aggressive and more infertile than most other men. Martins grow up to be parents of low birth weight babies.

Marvin

At best, a kid named Marvin will pick up the friendly, octogenarian nickname Marv. At worst, they'll call him Marvin.

Mason

I suppose in the thirteenth century to call oneself a Mason would be a source of pride. Now, it's like naming your kid Janitor.

Mateo

How a cat would pronounce Matt.

Matt/Matthew

A Matt is to be stepped on, and wiped with one's feet. Matthew sounds like a pretentious form of Matt—probably one of those Matts with fancy French designs.

Max

This name has traveled from humans to dogs and recently back to humans again. Consequently, many babies named Max can hear sounds normally undetectable to the human ear. They also shouldn't be around leather shoes when they're teething.

Maximus

WELL, WELL, WELL. AREN'T YOU EXPECTING A BIG BOY! MAXIMUS, GET ME MY SWORD AND WE'LL STORM THE GARRISONS.

Melvin

No one has actually used this name in fifty years, but if your son ever comes home after being called Melvin by his peers, you'll want to enroll him in self-defense class immediately.

Michael

Only John is more common in America. If a pre-birth IQ test, a lack of heavy kicking in the womb, or a series of uninspiring sonograms indicate that your son looks like he might not amount to much, this is the name for you.

Mitchell

They'll call him Mitch and he'll be everybody's pal. Mitch, the buddy. Mitch, the guy you can always count on for a good time. Mitch, who'll swipe your car on a Saturday night to take his buddies on a road trip to New Jersey, wrecking it on the way.

Morgan

Originally a Celtic name referring to those who lived near the sea. Of course the name takes on less significance when one considers that *everywhere* in Ireland you're near the sea! Apparently the connotation of the term is "one about whom there is nothing special."

Myles

A distance one might travel. For instance, many girls might brag about how far they would walk out of their way, say . . . five miles, to avoid a conversation with a dorky boy named Myles.

M

Neil

A name homonymous with lowering oneself in utter humility to another. Such children tend to be picked on rather easily but manage to get along as soon as they realize that their only means of survival is to abandon all dignity.

Nicholas

Ah, Nicholas. Evoking the beautiful images of Victorian England and jolly Saint Nicholas, who, as is popularly recounted every Christmas, fills a bag with presents and then breaks into your house to eat some of your food. He then starts up a relationship with your children by leaving them something from his big bag of toys. It's only a matter of time before that sick SOB gets caught.

Nick

Every morning women and men wince at the prospect of Nicks on their faces and legs. If they *get* a Nick, they invariably swear and curse the course the new day has already taken. Nobody wants a Nick. Nobody.

YOUR BABY'S SIGN

Babies born under this sign worship the Almighty Triangle and believe that upon its return to earth they will ascend to outer space.

Noah

Yes, ah. No, ah. Yes, ah. Of Biblical fame, the original Ted Kaczynski-ish loner. A man who had so few friends that he couldn't find a single other human (to whom he was not related) that he cared for enough to save from the flood. Among those he *did* save were a couple of cockroaches, a couple of rats, and a couple of slugs.

Nolan

Not actually a name, but some people with no concern for swiping the surnames off others' mailboxes and nameplates have been using this one to name their boys. Of course, it's not a first name and soon all boys named Nolan will be detained and renamed according to the desires of the state. Popular opinion guesses that the state will choose to rename them Smith.

Norman

NORMAN, defender of the average! Keeper of the median! Protector of the ordinary! Bitten by a radioactive bell curve while studying the effects of norms on invariable tangents, statistician Norm Vector suddenly becomes NORMAN, who, together with StandardBoy, fights the evil super-villain STANDARD DEVIANT and his maniacal plan to topple the balance of the world! Look! Up on a bell-shaped hill! It's a man. It's a man of average height and weight! It's NORMAN!

Oliver

Most famously the wimpy little British orphan with whom Dickens proves the point that rich people are honest—and poor people, especially those who are not Christian, are amusingly dishonest and deserving of their sad fate. Famous American Olivers (such as Oliver North and Oliver Stone) tend to be amusingly paranoid.

Orlando

Recently Orlando Bloom has transformed this handle into a swarthy, erotic name that on a suburban baby seems as ill-fitting as a silk diaper. Most babies named Orlando tend to grow sexy, waxed mustaches before they grow hair on their heads.

Oscar

Hilariously sloppy and grouchy, no matter who this name belongs to.

Owen

Many people tend to find boys' names starting with the letter O to be awkward and unattractive. With Owen, however, that trend is almost always inexplicably reversed. While Owen, the name, is aesthetically tolerable, Owen *babies* tend to be awkward and unattractive.

Parker

One who parks. No one exactly knows at what point in history valets achieved a societal rank so high that others would name their children in honor of them. Certainly, the days of the "glorious parker" and his many admirers have passed. Today he, along with the rest of the manual laborers, names his sons after great *modern* service occupations like Programmer and Exterminator.

Patrick

For Irish families who lack imagination and have already used Tommy, Patrick is the next obvious choice. In fact, those Irish families that do not name at least one son Patrick usually find upon leaving the hospital that their "Kiss Me, I'm Irish" bumper sticker has been ceremoniously ripped from their mini-van by angry leprechauns.

Paul

A name so common that even the biblical Paul can't stand it and changes his name to Saul. Now, nobody would voluntarily change his name to Saul unless he was really discouraged. That's what Paul'll do to a guy.

Payton

The greatest runner in NFL history and a truly inspiring human being; a man who never scored a Super Bowl touchdown and died in the prime of his life. Choosing this name is an excellent way to instill in your son an understanding that life simply isn't fair and exceptions aren't likely to be made for him.

Perry

A name created for soft and oddly shaped babies with thin skin who are easily spoiled.

Peter

In order to avoid the obvious diminutive phallic references, most parents will avoid calling their son Peter and will instead refer to him as Pete.

Phillip

Interesting fact: Even though Phillip has been in use for centuries, naming kings and janitors alike, never has a Phillip ever won a schoolyard fight. Somehow the name seems to have a degenerative effect on the development of muscles in young boys.

Pierre

In 2003, Americans everywhere were throwing perfectly good French wine down the drain to express their disgust for all things French. Of course doing so made no sense since they'd already purchased the wine, and in actuality were throwing their own wine down the drain. The moral of the story seems to be that some people don't need much of a reason to do something stupid. In such a climate, experts suggest that naming your baby Pierre might not be the nicest thing to do for him.

Preston

Old English surname referring to any one of many "priest towns" owned by the Church. It could also have referred to villages where the Church would cast off priests they found . . . irregular. Priests would be told they were to build a congregation in a new development, but, sadly, when they arrived, they'd find hundreds of other priests who'd been given the brush-off with the same story. Such towns eventually failed as everybody within them knew how to perform one's daily work in a godly manner, but nobody knew how to do the work itself.

Quentin

In Ancient Rome, parents would number rather than name their children. Quentin (or Quinten, or Quintus) would refer to the fifth child. Now, when parents name their first-born Quentin, they are risking embarrassing him . . . assuming he builds a time machine, travels back in time to ancient Rome, and tells everyone his name and how many siblings he has. Farfetched? Maybe, but at one time homes without vomitoriums probably seemed pretty farfetched, too—but according to *Martha Stuwardus Living* vomitoriumless homes are on the way!

Quincy

A suitable name for babies born with whiskers and fascinated by balls of yarn.

Quinn

The Irish version of "king," who despite his many holdings in the northern greenlands seems always to be after your Lucky Charms.

Ralph

As ugly as boys' names get. An interesting part of the evolution of this name is the fact that the verb "to ralph" (to throw up) came into being because so often the reaction to babies named Ralph was spontaneous vomiting.

Randall/Randy

Here are his choices: he can go with Randall and be the immediate enemy of every kid in fourth grade, or go with Randy and scare away teachers and babysitters.

Ray/Raymond

Yet another boy's name that means "king." You'd think with all these little kings walking around they'd be a little more concerned with geopolitical stability and a little less obsessed with PlayStation.

Reece

Likely nickname: Peanut butter. A name made especially popular of late with the rise of movie star Reese Witherspoon. Boys named Reece can expect to be one boy in a sea of girls named Reese. Early results have most boys giving in and just accepting their parents' wish that they become girls.

Reginald

No one actually seriously considers this anymore. Kind of a joke name that one might pretend to have chosen just to freak out the in-laws.

Reid

Celtic term for red. During the Cold War, this was not a particularly popular choice in the U.S.

Reuben/Ruben

A biblical name, first appearing as the eldest son of Jacob. As such, we could reasonably accuse him of being the mastermind behind the brutal plan to toss his brother, Joseph, into a pit and sell him to slavery. There's also a sandwich named Reuben (created by either Arnold Reuben or Reuben Kulokofsky, depending on who you believe). Reuben sandwiches are so offensively bad for you that researchers at the University of Nebraska claim that mice would rather smoke cigarettes than take a bite of a Reuben. Those mice that don't smoke will actually take it up in such situations.

Richard/Rick

You know the old saying: "When you can't get Dick, try Richard." Okay, it's not really a saying, but it's not a great leap from Richard, or any of its variants, to Dick. Indeed, Richard is really just a Dick in a turtleneck . . . (eew, let's try a different image). . . . Richard is really just a dressed-up Dick. But remove all the clothes, and what do you get? Dick. I say, if you want Dick, you should just go ahead and get it. Don't be afraid of what other people think. You like Dick. Good for you! But now have the courage to come right out and ask for it. Choose Dick and never look back.

Riley

While this name had almost vanished during the twentieth century, it has recently become a favorite of thousands of young parents paying tribute to iconic entertainer, *Match Game* contestant, and humanitarian Charles Nelson Reilly. Had Mr. Reilly not so amazingly dominated the cultural spotlight these past twenty years, this name might have disappeared long ago.

Robert

Your prospects look good. You hope to raise a Robert, handsome, strong, creative, and according to its meaning, destined for greatness. Unless, of course, he chooses to be called Bob—in which case he will be as ordinary as American cheese on white bread.

Rodney

Probably a derivation of the ancient Germanic name Roderick, which means "fame power." Fame Power is now the name of the most awesome superpower available to the Warhol Twins, two crime-fighting cartoon characters who, with their totally radical exploding press releases and flashing camera rays, stop crime in its tracks—or at least get it on TV. Unfortunately, Fame Power wears off in fifteen minutes. The most famous Rodney of the twentieth century achieved *his* notoriety by being beaten nearly to death by Los Angeles police. Fame has its price.

R

Roger

Here is a name that at one point commanded respect and implied sophistication; however, now the name is most often simply viewed as a synonym of "okay." Roger that?

Roman

Well, I hope you live in Rome. Because naming your child after a city you don't actually reside in just seems desperate. It's like those guys who live in Lithuania wearing Chicago Bulls shirts.

Ronald

A name inextricably linked with the world leader who changed the face of not only America but the rest of the world as well: Ronald McDonald.

Ross

A name that has grown in popularity over the past ten years, fueled almost entirely by mothers who claim that the greatest tragedy of the twenty-first century has been the canceling of *Friends*.

Roy

Yet another name that means "king." This is the French version and as such the king bearing this name is required to feed his people fancy *patisserie* items at the conclusion of each successful campaign.

Rudy

A name that boys just love having during Christmastime, when their friends amuse themselves by singing "Rudolph the Red-Nosed Reindeer" and squeezing little Rudy's nose until it bleeds.

Russell

Originally a French name referring to people with red hair, the name seems to have strayed far from its original intent. Now, Russells come in so many colors and sizes that the name hardly means anything at all. Like, it's just a bunch of random letters that don't mean anything at all. I'm glad it's not my name.

Ryan

Unlike so many boys' names that mean "king" or "ruler," Ryan actually means "little ruler." Kind of a mini version of an actual kid's name, like Rex or Roy. You could just call him MiniRex or MiniRoy. Nothing a short kid likes better than a diminutive nickname. I suppose it's better than naming him Shorty . . . but not much.

YOUR BABY'S SIGN

Babies born under this sign tend to befriend children inappropriately when they become adults.

R

From France to Freedom

In 2003, when France refused to take part in the removing of Saddam Hussein from power, thousands of Americans poured their French wines down the drain. The French, seeing wine that had already been paid for get absurdly wasted, claimed to find the whole affair funnier than "Jerry Lewis en *Le Professor Nuttiment*."

Not to be undumbed, Congress renamed items on its cafeteria menu, changing French toast and French fries to *freedom toast* and *freedom fries*. The French thought that amusing too, since neither item originated in France anyway.

The baby world suffered, however, as French names and variants that Americans had loved for years were recast to make them a little more patriotic and a lot less French.

French Name	American Revision
Andre	Democracy
Beau	Washington
Pierre	Fruitcake
Raymond	President
Amelia	Rifle
Bridget	Bridge
Camille	Camel

The Worst Baby Name Book Ever

French Name	American Revision
Celeste	Chevrolet
Frances	Freedom
Gigi	Prostitute
Marie	Apple Pie
Michelle	Van Halen
Noel	Christmas
Paris	Baltimore
Raquel	Rocky VI
Roxanne	Rocky VII
Simonne	Constitution
Suzanne	Independence

Salvador

Like boys named Chile, Iran, and Nicaragua, boys named Salvador stand little chance of ever becoming president since their names serve only to remind Americans of foreign policy disasters.

Sam/Samuel

While the biblical Samuel means "Name of God," this name has been revived in recent years as simply Sam, which in Old English means "half."

Sawyer

One who saws. Usually wood. I think this name has picked up in popularity due to an appreciation for Jesus's modest roots. However, it's worth remembering that Jesus didn't choose to go into the company business. As a matter of fact, there's absolutely nothing in the Gospels about Jesus hammering, prying, or even whittling.

Scott

For children who are bound to live in obscurity and poverty their whole lives, this name provides a glimmer of hope when they one day learn of an entire land dedicated to them, a land with all their favorite rides and cartoon characters within.

Sean

An absurdly spelled version of a name that in itself is an absurd misspelling of the least unique name ever. Essentially a sad attempt at trying to fit it. Like when a kid buys Abercrombie look-alike pants at Kmart, hoping to score some points with the ultra-conformist clique. The only thing sadder than desperately trying to fit in is *failing* at desperately trying to fit in.

Sebastian

A particularly popular name among future butlers and valets—those who will someday *serve* the rich.

Seth

This name is a terrific choice for parents who have recently overcome their lisps.

Shane

A cowboyin', steer ropin', s**t kickin', tobacco spittin' kinda name that is used almost exclusively by parents living in suburban subdivisions.

Shannon

As close as parents can get to slapping a gender identity crisis on their son.

Sheldon/Sidney/Stanley

The three old boys of the list. Sheldon, Sidney, and Stanley grew up together in the thirties, playing stickball and smelling of onions. A couple of years later, they fought side by side in Dubbaya Dubbaya Two, and even met some swell dames with great gams during their tour of Europe. One of the girls, a little French honey, told Stanley he was "the cat's meow," and Sheldon killed himself five lousy Krauts. The boys have traveled many years from those days, and they don't always agree on too much, but one thing Sheldon, Sidney, and Stanley can all agree on is that this country's "going to hell" and that damn rock 'n' roll music is to blame.

Silas

Ahoy, me matey! Silas be a name a landlubber might be proud to be a-signing with his scurvy hook. Aye, that it be!

Simon

Popular references include the effeminate little child in the bathtub and the effeminate big child on *American Idol*. One who names one's child Simon might find himself being accused of simony, a crime in which holy offices are bought and sold. However, to simonize a child would entail turning him over to be properly rust-proofed. A name that means so many things! And none of them have much to do with babies at all.

Skylar

Most parents who name their boys Skylar aren't quite ready to answer the question, "Really? His name is really Skylar?" as often as they end up having to.

Spence/Spencer

The proud history of this name goes back to the Middle Ages when Dispenser was the title given to one prestigious enough to work as custodian of the storage room. Kind of like the towel guy in today's locker rooms.

Steven

Greek term for "crown." While parents of Stevens believe this name is as kingly as any other, it is really just a reference to an article of clothing. Boys named Rex and Roy tend to want to place boys named Steven on their heads.

Stuart

Most boys named Stuart identify themselves early on in the school year by wearing bow ties and suits on the first day. Strangely, despite their clearly advanced intelligence, most Stuarts annually repeat the mistake.

Tanner

A holdout from the days when tanners of leather were so highly respected that they did away with their names entirely. Certain occupations today have yielded the same results. Consider these fellas, who may very well live in your neighborhood: Lever Puller, Dog Walker, and of course, Boat Washer.

Tate

The surname of a seventeenth-century English playwright who thought he could improve on Shakespeare's *King Lear*. He did so well that today none of his copies have survived.

Taylor

Years ago, the great "masters of alter-ation" (as they were often described) were held in such high esteem and respect that the wealthy villagers who employed them would name their children after them. Tailors couldn't afford names themselves and therefore resented these little aristocrats who bore the name Taylor. In retaliation, tailors would screw up the dry cleaning, losing pants and subtly dulling winter whites. Now that the needle arts have finally regained their universal preeminence, this name is becoming popular again.

Terrance/Terry

A name that began as a tribe of Romans whose name might be translated "from the Earth." Historians (okay, just me) speculate that the original holders of this name were particularly filthy and would make excuses for their poor hygiene by claiming to have actually grown out of the ground, like a potato or a carrot. Most other Romans didn't fall for that "bunkus," so the Terrances often found themselves odd man out on Orgy Night. Let that be a lesson to you.

Theodore/Ted

The sort of name that makes you itch when it rains. Ted feels like a checked coat over a suit jacket; like a $5 off coupon at a fine French restaurant; like shag carpeting and wood paneling.

Thomas

Guys named Thomas are notoriously skeptical (or doubting) and cheap, the sort of people who bring McDonald's coffee into a Starbucks or spend an hour divvying-up checks at dinner. Name your baby Thomas and be ready for him to reply, "Prove it!"

Timothy

A silly little name for silly little boys. Timmys are squealers and toadies. They grow up to be the sort of man who is happy to find a hair in his salad, just for something to complain about.

Toby

Of course, when all the baby boomers and everyone else who saw *Roots* dies, you won't have to worry about people associating your son's name with slavery. Until then, maybe you should just call him Kunta.

Todd

If this were not a name it would be the term to refer to any protrusion beneath the skin. It's always a good idea to have a doctor look at any Todd that should happen to show up.

Tony

Boys are often named Tony by parents who don't realize until after they've signed the papers that Tony is short for Anthony. Thus, due to the magic of genetics, boys named Tony just don't end up too smart.

Travis

A hee-hawin', good time havin', bronco bustin', Stetson wearin', boot stompin', manure shovelin', beer drinkin', wife beatin', convenience store robbin', police dodgin', time servin', parole violatin', trailer rentin', drug usin', alone dyin' . . . name.

Trent

Interesting facts about Trent: 1) No one named Trent ever worked in a factory. 2) The name Trent has never been embroidered on a bowling shirt. 3) Farmers instinctively avoid guys named Trent, as the only reason a Trent would set foot on a farm is to foreclose on it. Conclusion: Trents are slick and impressive. They just aren't known for working too hard.

Trenton

A name traditionally referring to towns rather than people (especially since it means "town by the stream"). Trenton evokes feelings of patriotism emanating from that glorious Christmas evening during the Revolutionary War when Washington threw custom to the dogs and ambushed the celebrating Hessians, letting them know just how dirty we were willing to play.

A Taunt for Every Child

In the American classic *Don't Name Your Baby* [1] (DNYB), I suggested that the only way to ensure your child a happy childhood was to not name him or her at all. Now, despite the over-whelmingly positive response to DNYB [2] from members of the scientific community, [3] I have decided to recant that stringent position. As I suggested in the introduction to this book, [4] most names are mediocre, boring, ugly, or forgettable because most people are mediocre, boring, ugly, or forgettable.

However, as a public service to all those parents who are still choosing names based on the degree of ridicule their child will receive in fourth grade, [5] I hope you will find the following list of taunts useful. The list was compiled from hours of observation in grammar school playgrounds throughout the country. [6]

Girls

Abigail/Abby – Scabby/Flabby

Agatha – Ragatha

Agnes – Her Fagness

Alyssa – Pissa

Amanda – Man

Amy – Lamey

Anna – Banana

Ariel – Scariel

Ashley – Trashly

Bianca – Binaca

Brooke – Crook

Callie – Collie

Carrie – Scary

Chastity – Chastity Belt

---

1. Available where all fine books are sold. Leather-bound edition for an additional $100.
2. Often referred to as "the book that defined a generation."
3. In this case, referring to a doctor friend who liked the book . . . well, actually just a veterinarian.
4. Yeah, it has an introduction. Think about reading it, would you? I didn't write it for my health, damn it.
5. And to help satisfy the minimum page requirement of my publisher.
6. Pursuant to a court order, the other does not "advise" that anyone hang around grammar school playgrounds, nor may he be found within 500 feet of said playgrounds.

The Worst Baby Name Book Ever

Drew – Spew
Eleanor – Smellanor
Elizabeth – Smellizabeth
Ella – Smella
Ellen – Smellen
Emma – Dumma
Erica – Scarica
Erin – Erin Go Braless
Esther – The Molester
Frances – Frank
Deena/Gina – Weenah
Grace – Gross
Hannah – The Banana
Hope – Dope
Jackie – Smacky
Jamie – Lamie
Jane – Plain Jane
Janet – Miss Jackson (if you're nasty)
Joy – The Boy
Judith/Judy – Booty
Kelly – Smelly
Keri – Scary
Leah – Good Leah

Leigh – Good Leigh
Lily – Silly
Mackenzie – Smackenzie
Maggy – Raggy
Melanie – Smelanie
Melinda – Smelinda
Melissa – Smelissa
Melody – Smelody
Monica – Harmonica
Morgan – Pipe Organ
Nina – Wina
Pam – Spam
Patty – Fatty
Ruby – Booby
Sheila – Banana Peel
Shelly – Smelly
Sherry – Scary
Skye – Skye the Guy
Stacy – Spacy
Tara – Guitara
Tina – Weena
Toni – Boney
Tori – Whorey

Boys

Adam – Madam
Albert – Fat Albert
Aldo – Dildo
Alexander – Salamander or
   Alexander the Geek
Aubrey – Audrey

Barry – Fairy
Blake – The Fake
Bob – The Knob/Blob
Brock – The Sweatsock
Brody – Grody
Bryce – Lice

Carter – The Farter
Chance – Underpants
Chaz – Spaz
Chris – The Priss
Clay – They just call him Clay.
   That's humiliation enough.
Clayton – Clayface
Cole – Hole
Curt – Dirt
Dallas – Phallus
Darrel – Carol
Darren – Karen
Dennis – The Menace
Denzel – Denzoil Peroxide
Dick – Uh . . . well, I guess just
      Dick.
Dirk – The Jerk
Doug – Slug
Drake – The Fake
Drew – Pooh
Dylan – The Villain
Earl – The Girl
Elijah – Smellijah
Eliot – Smelliot
Garrett – The Ferret
Gary – The Fairy
Graham – Cracker
Grayson – Gayson
Ian – Peon
Jack – Jackoff
Jake – The Snake
Jay – Gay
Jaylon – Gaylon

Jeremy – Germy
Kelly – Smelly
Kendall – Ken Doll
Kerry – Fairy
Kirk – The Jerk
Lance – Underpants
Lucas – Mucas/Pukas
Luke – Puke
Max – Maxi Pad
Mitch – The Bitch
Neil – Banana Peel
Nicholas – Pickleless
Noah – Blowah
Norman – Whoreman
Pat – Fat Pat
Perry – Fairy
Raymond – Gayman
Rob – Knob
Rudy – *1st Grade:* Dooty
   5th Grade: Booty
   8th Grade: Fruity
Russ – Puss
Ryan – Cryin' Ryan
Sam/Samuel – Spam
Scott – Snot
Tucker – [Do I need to spell it
out?]
Ty – Bow Tie
Uriel – Urinal
Victor – Sphincter

Trevon

This isn't really a name. Last year, a couple hundred people scrawled this on birth certificates when they were either dog-tired or drunk. It was kind of fun for a laugh at the time, but now these poor kids are stuck with the thing. I'm sorry for wasting your time.

Trevor

Your baby will be flying high with Trevor. For the refined newborn, neatly mustached and donning his snappy, vintage, leather flight jacket with luxurious lamb's wool lining, Trevor gives your boy that added je ne sais quoi, taking him from diapers to dapper.

Trey

A synonym of three. This name is perfect for the last born of a set of triplets. Name your child Trey and he'll probably spend the rest of his life in search of his missing siblings.

YOUR BABY'S SIGN

Babies born under this sign hate environmentalists.

Tristan

Strangely popular despite its sad meaning. Historians[1] often theorize that the name originated from an ancient custom[2] of determining at birth those sons most likely to disappoint their parents. Indications of these impending failures included low birth weight, poor lute tone, and an inability to earn a decent living by the age of five.

Troy

The doomed city that let itself be pulled into war with Greece over a girl that wasn't really that hot, was so stupid that they fell for the old Trojan horse bit, and today survives only as the name of a few suburbs and the most popular brand of condom. Boys named Troy tend to steal other people's girlfriends, fall for the exploding-snakes-in-the-can joke, and practice safe sex.

Tucker

This name, formerly only a surname, is really catching on in recent years. And why not? The noble field of tucking fabric may be gone, but the skills of a tucker ought to be celebrated and honored forever. Those guys in the Middle Ages, now they were some *real* tuckers. Their generosity was world famous, as many tuckers would provide, free of

---

1. In this case, the term "historian" should be understood as meaning "myself."
2. In this case, the term "ancient custom" should be understood as meaning "something I made up about the past."

charge, tuckings for their families. One cannot help but imagine with admiration the scene of a Tucker beneath his mother's dress, arranging her fabrics just so. So of course, it is in honor of these great "mother Tuckers" that you would name your son—a Tucker in name and a real tucker in heart.

Ty

Two letters? That's all you can spare for the kid? Just two lousy letters and one syllable? You must be a real tightwad! I'm glad you're not my mom.

Tyler

One who tiles. Certainly there was a day when people who tiled commanded such great respect and admiration among their customers that one of them would eventually name their child Tyler. These days, thankful parents are more likely to name their child something like Customer Service Representative or Cable Television Installer.

Tyrell

A strangely popular name that refers to any animal that stubbornly pulls at reins, such as a mule. Tyrell comes from the Greek *tyrannos* or tyrant, and the Norse of the Middle Ages would call a person Tyrell if he was so stubborn that nobody could stand him. In today's context, it'd be a little like naming your baby Jag Off.

Tyrese

The female version of Tyrell. For parents of twin boys, Tyrese can be used for the one that seems more effeminate.

Uriel

Honestly, "urine" came to mind long after I first heard this name. It'll never occur to a fourth grader. Don't you worry.

Victor

Victor, as in victory. Champion. Winner. When a baby comes into the world with a name that already implies they've won something, they tend to expect that sort of treatment all the time. Be prepared to be patting this kid on the back for even the most feeble efforts. Trophies and ribbons awarding participation have, no doubt, resulted from the popularity of this name.

Vincent

Means "conqueror." Many names have meanings that a child might not live up to, such as "handsome" or "king." That's okay though, since beauty is subjective and not every situation calls for a king. But conquering can take place in *any* situation. It's unlikely that little Vince is going to be too popular when he pulls off a daycare coup or celebrates a Little League baseball game by feasting on the bones of the other team.

Walter

Although the 2003 census claims that nearly 800 babies were named Walter during that year, no one can recall ever meeting anyone under fifty named Walter. Scientists theorize that babies named Walter age so rapidly that within a week of birth they are indistinguishable from actual fifty-year-olds. They complain of swollen prostates, worry about their investments, and fret that babies born the week after themselves no longer seem to have any values.

Warren

As close as you can get to naming your baby War without being ostracized by those less paranoid than yourself. This name shows up in great numbers among children of the Michigan Militia.

Wayne

Today's Modern Baby suggests the following gifts for babies named Wayne: historical nonfiction, barbeque aprons (try "I'm the Chef!" with a picture of a soot-covered cook who's apparently blown up the grill), and a mustache trimmer.

Wesley

Here's something interesting: Charles and John Wesley were the leaders of the Methodist movement. Their first names were Charles and John. Their *last* name was Wesley. *Last* name! Get it?

William

It seems that parents who name their kid William tend to be those who dislike the name Billy most. So why would they choose the *only* name that could possibly be altered as such? Maybe they just don't know—maybe they're just not very smart—maybe they are just daring tempters of fate; America's last great risk takers; lovers of the lusty lure of chance! Naw, they're probably just not very smart.

Willie

Perhaps the goofiest of all euphemisms for the male sex organ. I would think that if you were going to go that route, you'd choose something a little more dignified—like Dick.

YOUR BABY'S SIGN

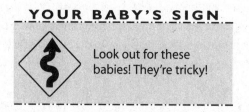

Look out for these babies! They're tricky!

Zachariah

A name that feels more comfortable on a '49 Gold Rush prospector than on a baby. If you name your kid Zachariah, don't be surprised to see him sporting red long johns and a white beard, panning for gold. Most mothers of Zachariahs report his first words as "Dag namit!"

Zach/Zachary

You can always spot the boys named Zach at a grammar school. Just go to the gymnasium and look for the boy at the end of the line. He'll be the one to get the most worn, under-inflated ball. Or saunter on by the cafeteria line, where Zach will be waiting for cold lasagna and stale fries, which he'll have to scarf down as fast as he can before the bell rings. Occasionally, a teacher will conduct business in reverse order, but Zachs will tell you that it can never make up for the daily indignities.

Zander

What is it that prompts parents to name their child Zander? The fact that a Zander is a type of fish? Or maybe they hope that when aliens land, little Zander will become instant friends with Emperor Xingdoid Zander of the red planet Zabulot.

Zane

Adjective, indicating the condition of sanity when assumed by a robot or any other mechanized being. Antonym: inzane.

Zion

Originally the name of a hill in Jerusalem; later the word meant all of Jerusalem. Then it meant all of Israel. Then it meant any perfect place. Now it's a name. Eventually, this word could mean just about anything! Are you willing to take that chance?